"Do any two elements of life go together mc[...]
encouragement? David Jeremiah offers both [...]
He can write about encouragement because he himself is an encourager.
He is qualified to offer hope because he is a man of Scripture. If hope is
lost and discouragement has set in, the *The Joy of Encouragement* is just
what the doctor ordered. Dr. Jeremiah's tonic is truth, and his prescription
powerful. A healthy dose of this volume will restore eternal hope and
emotional health. Highly recommended."

BRUCE WILKINSON, AUTHOR OF *THE DREAM GIVER* AND *THE PRAYER OF JABEZ*

"*The Joy of Encouragement* is just the spiritual tool you need to break down
walls, build bridges, heal wounds and get busy bringing hope to others.
People who want vitality and challenge in their lives will sing and shout
their way through this book. It's just the prescription we need for these
difficult days."

WARREN WIERSBE, AUTHOR OF *ON BEING A SERVANT OF GOD*

"A compelling call for us to infect our despairing and discouraged world
with hope and encouragement. This is a strategic book for those of us
who want to be used as helpers and healers on behalf of Christ.

JOSEPH STOWELL, AUTHOR OF *SIMPLY JESUS AND YOU*

"The land where 'seldom is heard a discouraging word' is most likely not
on planet earth. For so many folks, the 'skies are cloudy most of the day.'
They grow discouraged, lose hope, and need a road map home. David
Jeremiah's book *The Joy of Encouragement* provides the reader with practical, field-tested steps toward encouragement and hope. If you need a fresh
start, a new beginning, a renewed hope, then this is the book for you."

JOSEPH ALDRICH, AUTHOR OF *LIFESTYLE EVANGELISM*

"Read this book, and you will see the shrewdness of an investment in
encouragement. After all, it's a commodity always in short supply, and the
market gets stronger every year. David Jeremiah has written an encouraging word for folks who need encouragement and a helpful word on how
to be encouragers."

HADDON ROBINSON, AUTHOR OF *BIBLICAL PREACHING*

The Joy of Encouragement

Dr. David Jeremiah

Multnomah Books

THE JOY OF ENCOURAGEMENT
published by Multnomah Books

Published in association with the literary agency of
Yates and Yates
1100 Town & Country Rd., Suite 1300, Orange, CA 92868

International Standard Book Number:978-1-59052-703-0

Printed in the United States of America

Unless otherwise indicated, Scripture references are from
The Holy Bible: The New King James Version (NKJV) © 1984 by Thomas Nelson.

Scripture references marked TLB are from *The Living Bible,* © 1971 by Tyndale
House Publishers, Wheaton, Ill. Used by permission.
Scripture references marked Amplified are from *The Amplified Bible, Old Testament,*
© 1962, 1964, by the Zondervan Publishing House, or *The Amplified Bible, New
Testament,* © 1954, 1958 by The Lockman Foundation. Used by permission.

Published in the United States by WaterBrook Multnomah, an imprint of the
Crown Publishing Group, a division of Random House Inc., New York.

MULTNOMAH and its mountain colophon are registered trademarks
of Random House Inc.

For information:
MULTNOMAH BOOKS
12265 ORACLE BOULEVARD, SUITE 200
COLORADO SPRINGS, CO 80921

15 — 14

To the lay-shepherds of the
Twenty-Twenty Small Group Network
at the Shadow Mountain Community Church.
You have provided encouragement
for others and in the process
have greatly encouraged my own heart.

"I didn't skimp or trim in any way.
Every truth and encouragement
that could have made a difference to you, you got.
I taught you out in public
and I taught you in your home..."

Acts 20:20, The Message—Eugene Peterson

CONTENTS

ACKNOWLEDGMENTS

First, I owe a debt of gratitude to the members and friends of the Shadow Mountain Community Church. When I first taught the principles in this book to them, they encouraged me to put everything in writing. I am honored that John Van Diest wanted this to be one of the first books released by his new Vision House Publishing Company. Even though he was engulfed in getting his new venture up and running, he still took a personal interest in my book. That interest has continued with this new edition from Multnomah Books publishers, the "family" to which Vision House now belongs.

Sealy Yates is my friend and advisor, and he's the one who really put all the pieces together for the project.

Glenda Parker, who administrates my office, helped care for a myriad details that could have kept me from this assignment.

Finally, I express deep appreciation to my wife, Donna. Her encouragement keeps me going. More than anyone in the world, she believes in me and often tells me so!

"Love is the one ingredient of which our world never tires and of which there is never an abundance. The world will never outgrow its need for love."

C. NEIL STRAIT

WHAT THE WORLD NEEDS NOW

WHAT THE WORLD NEEDS NOW

Do you hear it? Listen carefully. Now do you hear it? No? Okay, then turn on your television—any channel will do. Now do you hear it? Still no? Well, it's there all right, but you might have missed it. Go to your front door and open it wide. Listen to the sounds in the streets. Did you hear it? Believe me, it is there!

This time close your door, turn off the television, and listen to the sounds in your own home. Do you hear it? To be certain, listen to your own heart. You hear that? Of course you do. It's unmistakable, coming through loud and clear: "I WANT TO BE LOVED." But wait, there's more. Listen closer: "AND I WANT TO LOVE."

A WORLD'S CRY

If you tune in to this world of made-in-the-image-of-God people, you will hear a cry to be loved and to love. These are two of man's most basic desires. We are shaped by those who love us or refuse to love us, and by those whom we love or refuse to love. Love is crucial! This is no news to God—He created us for love. And Jesus said our love for God and for our neighbor is the fulfillment of all the law of God.

The world cries out for genuine love, love which heals, unites, and encourages. Dr. Karl Menninger, famed American psychiatrist, found that people who are able to give and receive love recover more quickly from their illnesses. In contrast, individuals who lack love often develop personality scars and some even die.[1] Love is essential to our emotional, physical, mental, and social well-being.

In his best-selling book, *Games People Play,* Dr. Eric Berne discussed the tremendous human need for encouragement, by word and by touch, to keep their spinal cords from shriveling—to keep them alive, eager, and confident.[2] His book highlights the variety of games people devise to win this sort of healing attention.

Historian John P. Koster documents some experiments that demonstrated the severe impact on a child who feels unwanted:

> It's a well-known fact that children who receive an inadequate amount of love from their parents either die in infancy or grow up to be mentally and spiritually stunted adults. Stories about the absence of love are frequently found in literature beginning in the earliest days of history. In Herodotus, a Greek historian who wrote about 400 B.C., we find a narrative concerning Croesus, a fabulously rich king of Lydia, who performed an experiment in which he hoped to find out what the world's oldest language was. Croesus rounded up some unwanted babies, isolated them from all human contact, and had them suckled by female sheep until they learned to talk so that he could hear what language first came out of their mouths. According to Herodotus, though the children failed to thrive, they did survive, and they first uttered the word *bekos*. The king's courtiers couldn't agree whether this was an actual word or an imitation of the sheep.
>
> More than a thousand years later, according to a papal historian, the strange and mysterious German Emperor Frederick II decided to carry out the same experiment, but

this time the infants all died before they were old enough to speak because they had been deprived of human affection expressed through the stroking and cooing of their nurses.

FOUR LOVES EXPLAINED

Bartlett's Book of Quotations catalogs approximately thirteen hundred interpretations of the meaning of love as penned by poets, philosophers, and authors. Consider the many ways we use this word in everyday conversations.

I can remember hearing my children say, "I just love peanut butter and jelly sandwiches." Sometimes when a gift is appreciated, a person might respond, "I just love this new sweater." Mothers often coo, "I love you, sweet baby," to their newborn children. And when I'm away from home, I never end a telephone conversation with my wife without saying, "I love you!"

The English language uses the same word to describe our affection for peanut butter, sweaters, babies, and spouses. The word love means different things to different people. Fortunately, in the Greek language of the New Testament and the first-century world, four different words were used to describe four kinds of love.

Stergo (natural affection): This is the innate love we have for those in our families. "I love you because you are my sister."

Eros (self-serving passion): The word *eros* is not used in the Bible, but the concept is taught in books such as Song of Solomon. We get our word "erotic" from this Greek word. It's love for the sole purpose of sexual satisfaction. "I love you because you give me pleasure. If you stop giving me pleasure, I stop loving you."

Phileo (friendship): This is psychological, social love. It is often translated by the word "friend" in the Bible (see John 15:13–14). It speaks of the enjoyment we gain from another's company. "I like you because you are my friend and because of some of your qualities. This is a 50/50 relationship, you understand. If you don't give in return, or if there is much conflict, our relationship will end."

Agapé (giving of one's self): This is totally selfless love, a love which comes from and is rooted in God. *Agapé* is the power that moves us to respond to someone's needs with no expectation of reward. The fundamental attribute of *agapé* is sacrifice. So it's not 50/50, it's 100/0. "I'm going to give 100 percent even if I never receive anything in return. I will sacrifice even myself for you. I just want what's best for you."

EXALTED LOVE

Agapé is a love which comes from a God who is love. It is love lavished upon others without a thought of whether they are worthy to receive it. It is this kind of love that is to characterize the Christian.

> Beloved, if God so loved us, we also ought to love one another. No one has seen God at any time. If we love one another, God abides in us, and His love has been perfected in us. By this we know that we abide in Him, and He in us, because He has given us of His Spirit (1 John 4:11–13).

At least fifty-five times in the New Testament we are commanded to love. It is one of Scripture's most repeated, inescapable directives for the believer. It touches us in all of our relationships and affects us in each of the many roles we play—as parents, spouses, children, friends, and fellow believers. It even defines the way we are to respond to our enemies (see Matthew 5:43–44). Christ provided the crowning example of this when from the cross He prayed for those who were abusing Him. And Romans 5:8–10 tells us He died for us even when we were yet His enemies.

Believers are to follow the way of love (1 Corinthians 14:1), to do everything in love (1 Corinthians 16:14), to serve one another in love (Ephesians 4:2), to live a life of love (Ephesians 5:2), to speak the truth in love (Ephesians 4:15), to put on love (Colossians 3:12–14), to pursue love (1 Timothy 2:22), to spur one another on to love (Hebrews 10:24), and to love not only in words but in actions and truth (1 John 3:18). We are to be controlled by the Holy Spirit and to bear the fruit of the Spirit which is love (Galatians 5:22). And God is concerned that we grow and mature in this love. Three times in Paul's epistles and once in Peter's writings we are told to continue to grow in love.

LOVE: FACT OR FEELING?

Some may argue, "But love is a *feeling* and you cannot command a feeling. I just don't feel anything for him/her anymore." But *agapé* love is not primarily a feeling. God would not command a feeling. Love is primarily an action. Love is the giving of oneself to another. It's a skill one can develop in the strength of God's Spirit. "Love your enemies, bless those who curse you, do good to those who hate you, and pray for those who spitefully use you and persecute you" (Matthew 5:44). In other words, love insists we *do something*. Feelings for enemies are not developed by sitting in a dark room thinking, but by doing. Feelings follow action. Feelings are the fruit, not the root, of love.

If you give your enemy something to eat or drink, something happens to your feelings. When you invest yourself in someone, you begin to feel differently toward him or her. In his book, *None of These Diseases,* Dr. S. I. McMillen described how this works:

> When I quote the Bible to people who are suffering physi-cally or mentally from a lack of love, some of them retort that it is very difficult to change one's feelings, to change hate to love. That is true. Psychologists support this view, claiming that the will does not have complete control over the emotions. However, these same psychologists state that the will has good control over the actions. Our wills largely do have the power to decide what we do and what we don't do. This is fortunate because actions, over which we do

have power, can change our feelings. That's what Matthew 5:43–44 is all about. The action plan will work like Aladdin's lamp.

"Do good to them that hate you." Impossible? Not if you follow some easy directions.

Step #1: Walk out into your kitchen. Now you *can* do that. You have done it many times and you can walk there again.

Step #2: Make up a lemon meringue pie as delicious as one on a magazine cover…you have made your pie. So far so good! By that time you will feel a little better.

Step #3: Give your feet the sternest look they ever got, and inform them in a tone of authority, "Feet, you are going to carry me and this pie to Mrs. Quirks. Yes, I know you haven't been there in many a year, but you are going today."

Off you go. As you begin your adventure to seek the golden fleece of love, you feel strangely different. You feel warm, behind and a little to the left of your wishbone. You sense something wonderful is happening inside. Across the railroad tracks you go and down the dingy alley called Depot Street. You begin to understand Mrs. Quirks' attitude a little better as a noisy freight train passes, shaking houses and sidewalks, and the black soot soils your immaculate white gloves, and while dirty, boisterous children send shivers up your spine with shrieks and cursing. "Yes," you say, "if I had to live here, I think I would be irritable too."

As you go up the stairs, you cannot help smiling at the new role you are playing. You rap on the door and wait. To Mrs. Quirks' truly surprised look, you present your peace offering with a nice smile you decide to throw in for good measure.

A little chat in the living room, a cordial invitation for

her to visit you, then on leaving, a mutual hug and kiss—the fervor and spontaneity of it surprises both of you. You sense that a divine miracle has happened inside you because the love of God is truly coursing through your whole being. The impossible has happened!

On the way home you feel like skipping along the street, as you did when you were a carefree girl. Inside is the spirit of singing and summer, absent for many a year. You feel so good you decide not to stop at the doctor's to take that "shot" for frayed nerves. They aren't frayed anymore. You never felt better in your life. Even the pain in your back is gone.[3]

> He drew a circle that shut me out!
> Heretic, rebel, a thing to flout.
> But love and I had the wit to win.
> We drew a circle that took him in.[4]

What our world needs most is to see love in action—in our homes, in our churches, in our cities, in our streets. How can this happen? The solution is found in God's Word: "The love of God is shed abroad in our hearts by the Holy Spirit who is given unto us" (Romans 5:5).

"I WANT TO BE LOVED...AND I WANT TO LOVE." God hears these cries, and He wants to love this world through us by His Spirit. But remember, love demands action and we must take those first steps. We must put ourselves in situations where God can love through us. This book is dedicated to learning about one very practical, very powerful way to reach out to others with God's love.

Love this world through me, Lord
This world of broken men,
Thou didst love through death, Lord
Oh, love in me again!
Souls are in despair, Lord,
Oh, make me know and care
When my life they see,
May they behold Thee.
Oh, love the world through me.[5]

LOVE IN ACTION

The world today is reeling from disillusionment. Hordes of people are seeking answers—but precious few are finding them.

The world has no answers that satisfy (or even make sense) to people facing the kinds of tragedies we see all around us. The good news is that we who know God and His Son, Jesus Christ, needn't remain in hopelessness and despair. There *is* an answer—and His name is Jesus. That's not trite, theological church-talk. It's true.

Do you want to give hope to those around you? There's only one certain way and one sure source: Give them Jesus.

EVERYBODY IS A SOMEBODY

EVERYBODY IS A SOMEBODY

$\int$ everal years ago, the president of a Christian conference and cruise company called me with an invitation I couldn't refuse. "We're taking a cruise to the Caribbean and we're taking some bookstore owners," he said to me. "We thought at the last minute we ought to take a Bible teacher as well. Your wife can go! Won't cost you a thing. Can you do it?"

I called home and told my wife about the offer. I'll never forget her response: "If you didn't say yes, don't come home."

We went.

The ship was one of the largest cruise ships afloat. In the very center of the ship was a theater which seated five hundred people. The second night of the cruise, we attended a very professional, full-cast presentation of *My Fair Lady*. You may remember that this musical concerns the speaking of the English language. In the story, Professor Henry Higgins makes a wager with Colonel Pickering that he can take Eliza Doolittle, a Cockney flower girl, and change her patterns of speech so she could pass as European royalty. With Eliza boarding in the Higgins' home, the professor teaches and rehearses her for weeks until he has the confidence to put her to the test. He finally escorts her to a glittering event where she is completely accepted as royalty. She fools everyone.

But the story isn't over. Returning from the function, Higgins and Pickering relax in the living room and excitedly congratulate themselves on their tremendous accomplishment. All during this, Eliza stands in the shadows, watching them and listening to their boasts. Nobody pays any attention to her and she grows upset.

Finally Pickering leaves and Higgins says to Eliza, "Would you bring me my slippers?" But instead of bringing the slippers, Eliza gives him a piece of her mind. She tells him how angry she is and how badly they have treated her. She reminds him of how hard she has worked. But that isn't what really bothers her. She reverts to her Cockney accent and exclaims, "I will not be passed over!"

THE IMPORTANCE OF ENCOURAGEMENT

Eliza Doolittle's words speak for all of us. No one likes to be passed over. Something within each of us cries out to be noticed. Someone has suggested that most Americans suffer from a severe case of attention deprivation; we don't know if anybody really cares about us. Some of the Bible's saddest words are found in one of the Old Testament psalms when David cries out in a moment of extreme loneliness, "No one cares for my soul" (Psalm 142:4).

> "You learn to speak by speaking, to study by studying,
> to run by running, to work by working, and just so,
> you learn to love God and man by loving."
> SAINT FRANCIS OF SALES

In a cold world that refuses to recognize a loving God, words such as the psalmist's might be expected. But why do we hear these cries so often among believers? Is it possible that we have so focused our attention on those outside the church that we have neglected our responsibility to each other? God has given to us, His children, the solution to the lonely, hopeless heart. In His Body, the church, no one should be passed over. We are commanded to encourage one another.

The dictionary defines encouragement as the act of inspiring others with renewed courage, renewed spirit, or renewed hope.[1] In the New Testament, the word most often translated as "encouragement" is *parakalein*. This term comes from two Greek words: *para*, meaning "alongside of," and *kaleo*, meaning "to call." When people come alongside us during difficult times to give us renewed courage, a renewed spirit, renewed hope—that's encouragement. William Barclay helps us to understand the historical background of this word:

> Again and again we find that *Parakalein* is the word of the rallying-call; it is the word used of the speeches of leaders and of soldiers who urge each other on. It is the word used of words which send fearful and timorous and hesitant soldiers and sailors courageously into battle. A *Parakletos* is therefore an *Encourager*, one who puts courage into the fainthearted, one who nerves the feeble arm for fight, one who makes a very ordinary man cope gallantly with a perilous and a dangerous situation....
>
> The word *Parakalein* is the word for exhorting [others] to noble deeds and high thoughts; it is especially the word of courage before battle. Life is always calling us into battle and the one who makes us able to stand up to the opposing forces, to cope with life and to conquer life is the *Parakletos*, the Holy Spirit, who is none other than the presence and power of the risen Christ.[2]

Encouragement (*paraklesis*), often described and commanded in the New Testament, is an important character ministry for us to develop and practice. There are at least four reasons why we need to take our responsibility as encouragers very seriously.

1. It is the urgent need of our day

People often say we shouldn't be overly disturbed by the problems in our generation—we're just having the same old problems every generation has had. I used to believe that. I can remember expressing that theory to others: "Don't get so overwhelmed by your problems. They're not any different from the problems your parents had." Now, I know better.

The problems of this generation are far more complex than those of previous periods of history. Things people only toyed with in past generations have become epidemic today: Crime and prison crises, drug abuse crises, national debt crises, health care systems/Medicare crises, sexually transmitted disease crises (including AIDS), adolescent suicide crises, liability and litigation crises, ethics crises, and on and on the list goes.[3] These critical problems no longer grow a little bit each year; in the last decade, they have grown exponentially. And no one seems to have any real solutions! Listen carefully to the speeches from Washington: "We're going to fix problems A, B, and C." But we know that when these problems are fixed, a new group of new problems (problems X, Y, and Z) will be created.

Social critic Jeremy Rifkin complains:

Each day we awake to a world that appears more confused and disordered than the one we left the night before. Every time we think we've found a way out of a crisis, something backfires. The powers that be continue to address the problems at hand with solutions that create even greater problems than the ones they were meant to solve.[4]

Dr. Richard Swenson recalls one night when the fear and hopelessness of this generation became clearer to him:

A few years ago, I attended a late-night delivery by a very

young-looking twenty-two-year-old mother. As I was the faculty member "on call" and was simply assisting the resident with the case, I had not met the family before.

This was Brenda's first baby. She was acting bravely despite her obvious discomfort. An occasional cry escaped as the contraction peaked. Then she would close her eyes in exhaustion and await the next wave of pain.

The nurse who both coached and comforted Brenda would occasionally glance over to the window ledge where the husband sat watching television. Brenda had a long second stage of labor, and we were in the room for over two hours. But I never heard him utter a sound.

The resident and nurse were doing most of the work with the patient, so I just stood back and watched. Then I leaned against the wall and watched. Then I sat down and watched. I was tired. But despite my tiredness, I was also fascinated by the increasingly bizarre social event that was unfolding in the room.

It was around midnight. Brenda's labor happened to coincide with the end of one slasher-type movie and the beginning of another. The final hour of the first movie was filled with violence. I counted at least ten different extended sequences of knifings, bloody machine gun fights, and exploding cars and boats.

The nurse and I looked at each other and rolled our eyes in disgust. Should I use my authority to demand that the set be turned off? I thought about it for a while and then decided the husband might pull out his own submachine gun and blow me away. Anyway, the first movie was mercifully wrapping up, body bags all over the place.

By this time, the baby's head was crowning. Brenda was still fairly well controlled, but her cries were getting louder and lasting longer. Another ten minutes, I figured.

Still no response from the husband, who was settling in for the beginning of the next movie. On the television screen, a mother, father, and small child were strolling down a big-city street when they stopped to watch a clown act. Suddenly, one of the clowns grabbed the little boy by the hand and took off running across the street. With the boy yelling "Daddy, Daddy!" the clown leaped into the back of a waiting van, the father in pursuit. Just as the vehicle started to pull away, the father tore open the back door. The clown inside shot the father pointblank in the face. Blood was everywhere.

Just then—*exactly* then—Brenda screamed and the baby was born.

Go back inside, little one, I thought. *You really don't know what kind of world awaits you.*[5]

It's not hard for us to identify with Dr. Swenson. If you still have small children at home, you cannot help but look at what is happening in our world and wonder what the next two decades will bring. One thing's for sure: Our kids are going to need a great deal of encouragement. In fact, there has never been a time when the ministry of encouragement has been more crucial for the Christian family. Later on in this book we will devote entire chapters to the encouragement of our children and spouses.

I wear many hats as a parent, as all parents do. I am a provider, a leader, a disciplinarian when necessary. But I believe my greatest responsibility is as a cheerleader. More than anything else, kids today need the supportive love, encouragement, and cheering-on of their parents. James Dobson, the family expert who spent years studying problems of adolescent behavior, once said in my presence, "Here's the distilled wisdom of all my research. Here is what you need to do if you have adolescents: Just get them through it."

Just get them through it! Hang in there with them until the white-water rapids of the teenage years are left behind.

Encouragement is an urgent need of our day. A church which does not equip its people as encouragers will soon phase out of any meaningful ministry in its community. God help us to learn how to be encouragers!

2. It is the unique priority of our God

In the New Testament, each member of the triune God (God the Father, God the Son, God the Holy Spirit) places a priority on encouragement.

Paul wrote to the Corinthians, "Blessed be the God,...the Father of mercies [encouragement]" (2 Corinthians 1:3). Here Paul used the word *paraklesis*.

In one of his letters to the Thessalonians, Paul reminded his readers that Jesus Christ is also, at the very core of His ministry, an encourager (2 Thessalonians 2:16–17).

And what can we say about the Holy Spirit? "Encourager" is one of His names! The King James Bible says of the Holy Spirit (in John 14 and 16), "However when He the Comforter is come...." The title "Comforter" translates the word *paraklete* which means "to encourage." When we encourage people, we live out the ministry of the third Person of the Trinity. He is *the* Encourager.

God the Father encourages. God the Son encourages. God the Holy Spirit encourages. We need to be encouragers because encouragement is one of the primary ministries—in fact, it's a priority—of our triune God.

3. It is the underlying purpose of our Bible

Many modern churches are driven by market research. Market research shows how to grow churches by determining, among other things, what people want to hear. According to most researchers, people want to hear things that make them feel better.

Many churches claim their rapid growth has resulted from market research.

But if a church "pep talk" is not based on the Word of God, it's short-lived. People can leave the service all "pumped up" and encouraged, but when the message doesn't provide the staying power for the inevitable times of stress, people can lose faith in themselves and in those who delivered the message. The result: a person is "downer" (when they come off their "upper") than they were before.

Fortunately, the Bible is filled with encouraging truth. There's no need to find substitutes from other sources. God's Word is filled with truth, given to us for the sole purpose of encouraging our hearts. In Romans 15, Paul reminds us that one of the purposes of the Old Testament was to provide encouragement for us today: "For whatever things were written before were written for our learning, that we through the patience and comfort [encouragement] of the Scriptures might have hope" (Romans 15:4–5). Everything from Genesis to Malachi was written for our learning, so that we, through the encouragement of the Scriptures, might have hope. If you don't get your encouragement from God's Word, you may find its benefit sadly temporary.

> "We live by encouragement and we die without it, slowly, sadly, and angrily."
>
> CELESTE HOLME

In the New Testament, the theme of encouragement is everywhere, especially in Paul's writings. When Paul wrote to Timothy and Titus, he reminded those young pastors of the critical importance of using God's Word as a tool of encouragement. "Preach the word! Be ready in season and out of season. Convince, rebuke, exhort [encourage], with all longsuffering and teaching" (2 Timothy 4:2).

In 1 Thessalonians 4, Paul told the Thessalonian believers to be confident about their future with God in heaven. He told them how future events would transpire and how Christ would come back for His own. Then, after delivering this great teaching about future hope, Paul said, "Therefore, comfort [encourage] one another with these words" (4:18).

In 1 Thessalonians 5, Paul spoke of the Day of the Lord which would come like a thief in the night. When he finished teaching about this great prophetic truth, he said, "Therefore, comfort [encourage] each other and edify one another, just as you also are doing" (5:11).

One of my highest goals as a pastor is that my flock, by the grace of God, will leave every Sunday with encouragement in their hearts—not from something cute I conjured up, but because I pointed them back to the solid encouragement found in the Scriptures. People are encouraged by the Word of God.

4. It is the uncommon opportunity to begin a never-ending process

Encouragement is like a pebble thrown into water. While there is always an immediate impact, the ripples continue indefinitely. Paul spoke of this when he wrote to the Corinthians, "I want you to know how blessed I am by the God of all encouragement who encourages us so that we in turn can encourage others with the encouragement whereby we ourselves have been encouraged" (2 Corinthians 1:3–4, my paraphrase).

When you have been encouraged, your first impulse is to encourage someone else. Encouragement is infectious. The only way you can truly appreciate the encouragement you have been given is to give it daily to another. That person will in turn hook up with someone else who needs a word of affirmation, and the ripples continue to grow. Encouragement begins a process which should go on forever.

A ROUND-TRIP ENCOURAGEMENT

Throughout my years of preaching, I have often mentioned the name of Joseph Bayly. Joseph was a bold and creative writer who made a great contribution to his generation by courageously addressing the subjects of suffering and death. In my opinion, his personal qualifications for such difficult assignments are unmatched by any other author.

Joseph Bayly buried three sons: An eighteen-day-old infant; a five-year-old victim of leukemia; and an eighteen-year-old who died of hemophilia complications after a sledding accident. Joseph's books, *The View from the Hearse, The Last Thing We Talk About,* and *Heaven* grew out of his bitter exposures to death.

Shortly before the eighteen-year-old died, he became engaged to a very godly young woman. After his death and in the midst of her own sorrow, this young woman was deeply concerned about the sorrow of Joseph Bayly and his wife. She gave them a poem which had meant a great deal to her, verses written by German pastor Dietrich Bonhoeffer titled "Next Year—1945." Bonhoeffer had written it for his own fiancée just three months before he was taken by the Nazis and executed at the age of thirty-nine. He wrote the poem while in jail during World War II. The poem was delivered to his fiancée after his death; she was responsible for its publication. Two of the seven stanzas read as follows:

Should it be ours to drain the cup of grieving,
even to the dregs of pain, at thy command,
we will not falter, thankfully receiving all that is given by
thy loving hand.

While all the powers of Good aid and attend us,
boldly we'll face the future, be what it may.
At even, and at morn, God will befriend us,
and oh, most surely on each new year's day![6]

When Joseph Bayly wrote his book on heaven, he included this poem in his book. Twelve years after the death of Joseph's oldest son and thirty years after Bonhoeffer's death, the Baylys received a letter from a young pastor in Massachusetts. This pastor told of visiting a woman in a Boston hospital who was seriously ill. On one of his visits the pastor gave her a copy of Joseph's book, *Heaven*. The woman stayed up all night reading it. The next day she told of the comfort and help it had brought her. Within a few days, she died.

This woman had immigrated from Germany shortly after the war. Her name was Maria Von Wiedermeier. At the time when Bonhoeffer was imprisoned and executed, she was Bonhoeffer's fiancée. From Bonhoeffer to Maria, from Maria to another grieving fiancée, from this fiancée to the parent of the one she loved, from one of his books to other hurting people, then through a friend of his back to Bonhoeffer's Maria as she lay dying in a Boston hospital.[7] Ecclesiastes says, "Cast your bread upon the waters, for you will find it after many days" (11:1).

My friend, when you give away encouragement, you start a ripple effect. You never know what will happen with that kind word, that written note, that warm touch you give to a grieving, hurting person. You could start something that will never end.

LOVE IN ACTION

Two of the most talented songwriters of our time are Bill and Gloria Gaither. What a multitude of marvelous songs have come from their hearts and their dedicated minds! Both enjoy a marvelous Christian heritage that plays such a dominant role in their spiritual lives and daily activities.

In the late 1960s, while expecting their third child, the Gaithers were enduring a traumatic time. Bill was recovering his strength from a bout with mononucleosis; they (along with their church) were the objects of accusation and belittlement; and Gloria was understandably fearful of bringing children into such a crazy, mixed-up world.

As Gloria sat alone in a darkened living room—tormented, fearful, and thoughtful—the Lord knew her need and suddenly sent to her a calm and peaceful rest. The panic left and was replaced by a peace that surpasses all understanding, an assurance that the future, left in God's hands, would be fine.

The presence of the Holy Spirit was particularly precious as the Gaithers remembered that His strength and power were at their disposal. The power of the resurrection of Christ seemed to affirm itself in their lives once more. Gloria remembers thinking that "It was LIFE conquering death in the regularity of my day." The joy seemed to overcome and supersede frightening human circumstances.

In her book, *Fully Alive,* Gloria relates what took place shortly after that marvelous experience:

One day in the late fall, we had some men come to pave the parking lot behind our office. They brought load after load of coarse rocks, pea gravel, and sand. They brought huge, heavy rollers and smashed all of that down. Again and again they rolled it. Finally came the streaming truckloads of molten asphalt to be poured atop the gravel, then rolled again and again until it was smooth and hard and "permanent."

Very early the next spring, Bill's dad came into the office one morning, and stood around on first one foot then the other, grinning as he does when there's something special on his mind.

"Come out here," he finally said to Bill and me. We followed him out the back door onto the shining new pavement. Right in the middle of it he stopped and pointed, "Look, there."

Up through the sand, up through the gravel, up through the rocks, up from the darkness and through the thick layer of asphalt had pushed a green shoot. It wasn't tough, it wasn't sharp, it wasn't strong. Any child could have plucked it up with nearly no effort at all. But it was alive! And there it stood, bright green in the sunlight, boasting to the world of its photosynthetic miracle: life wins!

There wasn't much to say. We just smiled our message of reassurance at each other; but I couldn't help thinking of the song we had just written after our own personal bout with darkness:

God sent His Son; they called Him Jesus.
He came to love, heal and forgive.
He bled and died to buy my pardon;
An empty grave is there to prove
MY SAVIOR LIVES.
How sweet to hold our newborn baby,
And feel the pride and joy he gives;
But greater still the calm assurance:
Our child can face uncertain days
BECAUSE HE LIVES.

Because He lives
I can face tomorrow!
Because He lives
All fear is gone!
Because I know
He holds the future,
And life is worth the living
JUST BECAUSE HE LIVES![8]

A RESURRECTION OF HOPE

A RESURRECTION OF HOPE

Jerusalem reverberated with the aftershocks; Jesus of Nazareth had just been crucified. It was national headline material. Everyone knew about the execution and everyone had an opinion about the late homeless prophet from Galilee. His death relieved many; His presence in the temple city had disrupted and traumatized their lives. Now, with His passing, they could go on with their normal, everyday living. They could proceed with another normal, every-year Passover feast.

For others, however, His death meant mourning and despair. Grief flooded their hearts—not the grief exhibited over the death of a loved one, but the despair associated with the death of a national hero (even a would-be national hero). You see, they had *believed* in Him. They had believed He was the Messiah. They had believed and hoped and trusted that He was the coming deliverer who would free them from Roman domination. But the Object of their hopes had been lifted up on a cross and forced to hang there until dead by the hand of the very Roman Empire He was supposed to conquer. Then He had been placed in a tomb; and as far as His mourners knew, there was no bringing Him back. Their

Hope was gone. He was dead. And so they were devastated, in shock.

But then, on the third day, the stories began to circulate. His body was not where it had been laid! Many were saying He had risen from the dead. People reported seeing Him—ten reports altogether, and five of them in a single day.

Early on the first Easter Sunday, He appeared first to Mary Magdalene, then later to the women who were returning to the tomb. Soon after that He showed Himself to ten of the disciples assembled in an upper room, also to Peter in a private appearance. But the fifth appearance was perhaps the most astonishing of all.

ON THE ROAD TO DESPAIR

On that first Easter afternoon, as the sky darkened toward dusk, Jesus appeared to two men who were traveling from Jerusalem to Emmaus, a two-hour journey of a bit over seven miles. These two men were disciples of Jesus. They were probably among the seventy-two men Jesus sent out to "heal the sick…and say to them, 'The kingdom of God has come near to you'" (Luke 10:9). They were with the Eleven (the Twelve minus Judas), to whom Mary Magdalene and the other women came with the incredible news that Jesus' tomb was empty and was being guarded by two angels who told them Jesus had risen from the dead. And do you know what? Nobody believed them. The text states, "and their words seemed to them like idle tales, and they did not believe them" (Luke 24:11). Peter and John went to investigate the tomb, but everyone else remained behind. Two of the disbelievers were the pair of men

> "O my soul,
> why be so
> gloomy and
> discouraged?
> Trust in God!
> I shall praise him
> for his
> wondrous help;
> he will
> make me smile
> again,
> for he is my God!"
>
> PSALM 43:5, TLB

who were traveling to Emmaus that day. They had heard the witness of the women, yet they held onto their doubt and their sadness.

Why the journey to Emmaus? We don't know for sure. But I can imagine they took the trip to get away from it all—to escape Jerusalem's hopelessness, to clear their minds, to return to their homes and think about a new direction for their lives. That's the human angle. But evidently God had a different purpose in mind. For on the way, they would be intercepted by a mysterious stranger—and because of this encounter, they would never be the same. What started as a physical journey quickly became a spiritual one as well.

Interestingly enough, the most detailed record of any of Jesus' post-Resurrection appearances doesn't involve Mary, Peter, or any of the known disciples. It involves two unknowns, two men who are not specifically mentioned up to this point in the Scriptures. Cleopas makes his debut in Luke 24, while the other traveler goes unidentified. As I studied this, I couldn't help but think, *It would be just like Jesus to do that*. He is not partial to the well-known. He does not gravitate toward the famous. He comes to the meekest and the weakest of us, to bring His joy and gladness into our lives.

THE THREE-ACT DRAMA

Luke 24:13–35 may be one of the most dramatic presentations in the whole New Testament. In essence, it's a three-act play. Act One takes place on the road between Jerusalem and Emmaus, with the stage occupied by only two players, Cleopas and his friend. Act Two, also on the road, begins when a mysterious stranger joins them. And Act Three takes place in a humble home in Emmaus as the three prepare to share a meal.

Act One: Discouragement

Discouragement seems to have three levels. *Doubt* comes first. These two disciples had heard the testimony of Mary Magdalene and the other women, yet they did not believe. *Disappointment* naturally followed. Verse 21 spells out the cause of their gloom: "We were hoping that it was He who was going to redeem Israel." All of their dreams for the future had been crucified with Jesus. They probably had heard from the Eleven that Jesus stated, "I am the way, the truth, and the life. No man comes to the Father except through Me." They believed He was the Messiah, the fulfillment of all of the Old Testament prophecies. Yet now this One in whom they had invested all of their hopes had been taken to a cross and crucified. For all they knew, He was still dead—despite the rumors, despite the stories.

Their discouragement didn't stop with doubt and disappointment, however. It spiraled down even further until it reached the point of *despair*. All hope had been abandoned; three days had passed since the crucifixion. There had been no credible news upon which to pin any new hope. So, as they walked back toward Emmaus, they were overwhelmed with discouragement. Verse 17 says their faces were "downcast." One writer has summed up their emotional state this way:

> But Cleopas and friend had a problem. They were bitterly disappointed and disheartened. The nails driven through Jesus' hands and feet had punctured their belief and their hopes were leaking out. Just when they...concluded that Jesus was the Messiah, they were...[now] computing that nothing had been what it seemed. They could make no sense of the available data. There could be no explanation plausible or powerful enough to lift their heavy despondency.[1]

Act Two: Dialogue

All of a sudden, in what appears to be the moment of their greatest despair, the mysterious man appears. The text says that He "drew near." This New Testament expression conveys the idea that Jesus had been walking behind them and quickened His pace until He caught up with them. Instead of two, now there were three!

Cleopas and his friend had been discussing how their hopes had been dashed by Jesus' crucifixion. At that very moment, the Topic of their discussion joined them on the road and entered into their conversation. The men confessed their knowledge of Jesus. They believed He was a prophet. They talked about His mighty works. They called Him a Redeemer. (It's surprising how much you can believe without believing enough!) They hailed Him as a miracle worker. But they had not yet processed the one thing they needed to believe—that He had risen from the dead.

I feel obligated to say right now that it's possible to be a Christian and not *understand* the resurrection. Yet it's not possible to be a Christian and *disbelieve* in the resurrection. If Jesus Christ did not come out of the grave victorious over death, then He did not tell the truth; and if He did not tell the truth, He cannot be God. First Corinthians 15:17 tells us, "If Christ is not risen, your faith is futile; you are still in your sins!"

These two disciples had believed everything except the essential thing. They believed Jesus was a good man, a prophet, a redeemer, a miracle worker. Yet He said He had to rise from the dead, and they did not know that He had done that very thing! They were discouraged and sad. As they discussed recent events, Jesus spoke up and said, "What kind of conversation is this that you have with one another as you walk and are sad?" (Luke 24:17). This is how the men answered (my paraphrase): "You must be the only stranger in Jerusalem who doesn't know about these things. Where have you been, Mister, that you don't know what's going on?" Then Jesus inquired: "What things?"

Have you ever wondered why He asked such a question? My guess is He wanted to draw from them what He already knew they were thinking. As He had done so often with the Twelve, He wanted to expose their lack of faith. But even more than that, I think Jesus was giving us, the future readers of this account, an example of how to deal with people steeped in disbelief. He naturally walked with them. He easily conversed with them. Only at the appropriate moment did He open the Scriptures to them.

"Beginning at Moses and all the Prophets, He expounded to them in all the Scriptures the things concerning Himself" (Luke 24:27). People sometimes say, "You can't learn about Jesus from the Old Testament. You must learn about Jesus from the New Testament." Please observe: Jesus preached about Himself through Moses and the prophets—that is, from the Old Testament. Serious students of the Bible understand that the Old Testament is a picture in advance of the Messiah, who is presented in detail by Matthew, Mark, Luke, and John.

> "Why are you looking in a tomb for someone who is alive? He isn't here! He has come back to life again!"
>
> LUKE 24:5–6, TLB

Wouldn't you love to know what Jesus said when He opened the Scriptures and taught concerning Himself? I've often wondered what passages He used. Did He tell the story of Abraham and Isaac on Mt. Moriah? Did He preach the gospel from Isaiah 53:6? "All we like sheep have gone astray; we have turned, every one, to his own way; and the Lord has laid on Him the iniquity of us all."

As the threesome neared the turn-off to the village of Emmaus, Jesus acted as if He were going farther down the main road. But Cleopas and his friend insisted that Jesus go with them into Emmaus and stay with them for the night. The Master agreed, and together they walked toward the village.

Act Three: Discovery

When they arrived at the home (probably of one of the disciples), they sat down for an evening meal. "Now it came to pass, as He sat at the table with them, that He took bread, blessed and broke it, and gave it to them. Then their eyes were opened and they knew Him; and He vanished from their sight" (Luke 24:30–31). Jesus opened up the Scriptures to them and He opened up their eyes so they could see. But it wasn't the opening of the Scriptures or the opening of their eyes that caused them to recognize Jesus. Verse 35 tells us, "He was known to them in the breaking of bread." They discovered it was Jesus when He broke bread for the evening meal.

Remember, the two men had been on a long journey and it had been a long day. They were emotionally spent. They came in, sat down at the table, and Jesus took over. It wasn't His home, yet He broke custom by distributing the food. He asked the blessing. He presided over the meal, even though He was a guest. He took the bread, began to prepare it, broke off a couple of pieces, and handed them to the men.

Cleopas and the other man looked down, took the bread out of Jesus' hand—and what did they see? A nail print. Can you imagine their reaction? I wonder what they said? I can just imagine Cleopas turning to his friend and exclaiming, "Look! Look! It's Him! The One about whom we have talked is here in our home with us, Himself!" Then, just as quickly as He had joined them on the road, He vanished from their sight.

Just think of the incredible change which took place within the hearts of these men. Consider their feelings at the beginning of the journey. Recall the Bible lesson they received. Imagine seeing the Resurrected Christ. Just a few hours earlier, they were ready to give up on life; their hopes were gone. Now watch what happens.

A CHANGE OF HEART

These men had endured a long day of travel. They were preparing to feed their physically and emotionally exhausted bodies. Then Jesus vanished. And then? And then they were so energized that they got up and made the trip back to Jerusalem that very night— seven-plus miles—to find the disciples!

"And they said to one another, 'Did not our heart burn within us while He talked with us on the road, and while He opened the Scriptures to us?' So they rose up that very hour and returned to Jerusalem, and found the Eleven and those who were with them gathered together" (Luke 24:32–33).

An hour before, they wouldn't have had the energy or the desire to make such a trip. But now, after seeing Jesus and being encouraged by His presence, they were ready to fly! Back to Jerusalem they went. They found the disciples and told them about their life-changing experience. He was alive! He had risen from the dead! The Bible says He opened the scriptures (Luke 24:31). then in Luke 24:35 we see He opened their mouths! And they couldn't stop talking about the One they had seen.

FREED FROM THE GRAVE

I have always been a fan of Alfred Hitchcock. In one of his classic TV episodes, he dramatized the story of a wicked woman who had been convicted of murder and sentenced to life in prison. In a courtroom scene, the angry woman screamed at the judge and vowed that, no matter where she was imprisoned, she would escape and come back to make him sorry that he had sentenced her.

Guards removed her and she took that infamous bus ride to prison. En route, she noticed something which was to become part of her escape plan. She saw an old man, a prison inmate, covering up a grave outside the prison walls. She soon realized the only way she could escape was to get a key to the prison's gate. And the only inmate who had a key was the old man who assisted in the burial of dead prisoners. In fact, he not only buried them, but he also built the caskets in which they were buried. His job included rolling the casket onto an old grave cart outside the walls, lowering it into the hole, and covering it up with dirt.

This old man was going blind and needed cataract surgery. The woman discovered this fact and approached the old man, telling him that if he would help her escape, outside the walls she had enough money to pay all of his medical expenses. He could have his eyes completely fixed.

At first, he said, "No, ma'am. I can't do that."

"Oh, yes, you can," she replied. "Outside of this place, I have all the money you need to pay for your cataract surgery. If you help me get out of here, I will give you that money. If you ever hope to have an operation, you will help me escape."

Finally, the man reluctantly gave in. Here was the plan. The next time she heard the toll of the bell which signaled the death of an inmate, she would slip down to his workroom where he made his caskets. She was to locate the casket in which the old man had placed the corpse, then secretly slide herself into that same casket and pull the top down tightly. Early the next morning, the old man would roll her along with the corpse in the casket, out to the place of burial. He would drop the casket into the hole, dump a little dirt on it, and the next day he would come back, uncover the grave, release the lid on the casket, and she would be free.

A perfect plan…almost.

Late one night she heard the toll of the bell. Someone had died. This was her moment! She secretly slid off her cot and made her way down the hallway. Looking into the dimly lit room she saw the casket, and without hesitation she lifted the lid and in the darkness slipped into the box. After squeezing in beside the corpse, she pulled the lid down tightly. Within a matter of hours she could feel herself being rolled to a grave site. She smiled as the casket was placed in the hole and clumps of dirt began to hit the top of the casket. Before long, she was sealed beneath the earth. Yet she smiled. In fact, she couldn't contain her excitement. She had done it!

Time began to drag. The next day came and passed into the night and still the old man didn't show up. Now she began to worry. Where was he? What could possibly have gone wrong? Why hadn't he shown up? She broke into a cold sweat.

In a moment of panic, she lit a match, glanced at the corpse next to her and discovered...the old man himself. Her only hope lay buried right beside her.

THE ENCOURAGEMENT OF THE RESURRECTION

The greatest encouragement man will ever know is the giving of Jesus Christ to our world. Through His death, burial, and resurrection, Jesus has written the word HOPE in every heart. Because He lives, we too shall live. Because He was victorious over death, our future is bright.

Songwriters Bill and Gloria Gaither captured this thought when they wrote these words:

Because He lives, I can face tomorrow;
Because He lives, all fear is gone;
Because I know He holds the future,
My life is worth the living,
just because He lives.[2]

As we consider the encouragement of Christ's resurrection, we should respond in two definite acts of love. Both of these responses are illustrated for each of us by the great apostle Paul. They are recorded in the last two verses of 1 Corinthians 15, the Bible's great resurrection chapter.

First, we should express our gratitude to our Father in heaven:

"But thanks be to God, who gives us the victory through our Lord Jesus Christ" (1 Corinthians 15:57).

And second, we should do as Paul did—use the truth of Christ's resurrection to encourage others: "Therefore, my beloved brethren, be steadfast, immovable, always abounding in the work of the Lord, knowing that your labor is not in vain in the Lord" (1 Corinthians 15:58).

Think of it: Both victory and fruitful labor for us, all because of the resurrection. Cleopas and his friend enjoyed both benefits almost 2,000 years ago when Jesus broke bread with them, and it changed their lives. The same benefits are offered to us today, packing the identical life-changing power.

And all it takes is having your eyes opened to the risen Jesus.

LOVE IN ACTION

It is the resurrected Jesus who equips you to encourage others. Read these words from Stephen Hopper and allow the Lord to use you as an encourager.

Have you noticed that often it is the timing of a thoughtful gesture, rather than its scope, that makes the difference?

For a lonesome serviceman or woman, that refreshing lift could be a timely letter or a card. For a frazzled couple with young children, it could be an offer to baby-sit so they can go out for an evening or a weekend get-away. For a discouraged Christian worker, it could be a weekend at a conference or a retreat. For an elderly person or shut-in, a card, a call, or a visit could be the highlight of the week. For a student feeling pressured and homesick, it might be an offer to go out to lunch, or to help study for an exam. For a frustrated Sunday school director who can't seem to find anyone who will help, it could be an offer to fill in wherever you're needed most.

The ministry of refreshment involves genuine concern, willingness to take risks, and persistence in service. It requires being alert to the needs of others and seeking to provide relief from the pressures that burden them.[3]

The Lord has promised that those who hope in Him shall gain new strength and be renewed (see Isaiah 40:28–31). He may use a supernatural means to fulfill this promise. Is it possible, though, that He might want to use a human instrument? Might He want to use…you?

WHEN ALL ELSE FAILS

WHEN ALL ELSE FAILS

In 1981, a small, six-seat Cherokee plane carrying five people crashed into a remote ridge in one of the most rugged ranges of Colorado's Rocky Mountains. Gary Meeks, a Dallas construction worker, piloted the plane. He was accompanied by his wife, two sons, and a former business associate. Gary was headed to Aspen for a long-anticipated skiing vacation when, without warning, the plane began to lose power and crashed into the snow-covered mountain. The snowpack cushioned the impact, however, and all the passengers survived. The crash prompted one of the most extensive search missions in Colorado history. Yet how do you find a white airplane lost on a mountain covered with white snow? During the long and agonizing wait for the search party, Gary Meeks kept a diary of his thoughts:

> It took all afternoon today to clear away my head. I was so groggy, every time I looked out the window of the wrecked plane at the mountainous granite walls, all half-hidden behind a veil of blowing snow, I could just think in my heart, *this has to be a bad dream*. But then I would look around at Pat and the boys, their faces filled with fear,

shivering in the frosty cabin, and I realized again what had happened.

I don't remember the crash. All I know now is that my shoulder is separated. It's cold, cramped, I'm in pain. I wonder if anybody else knows we've crashed. No matter. There's nothing else for us to do but to just sit here and wait.

But what a moment today! Arne was cleaning out a suitcase. He was going to fill it with snow and bring it back in the cabin so we would have snow to eat. When he cleaned out the suitcase he found his Bible. I never have been so thrilled about a Bible before. We all took turns in that cold cabin trying to read little pages out of that book, while trying to keep our spirits together. This morning two planes flew over, but I'm sure they didn't see us.

It's so cold, and hope is so hard to find. I heard it shortly before daylight. It was a low, throbbing sound in the distance. It was coming closer. It was a rhythmic thub, thub, thub. Unmistak-

> *"Plant a word of love heart-deep in a person's life. Nurture it with a smile and a prayer, and watch what happens."*
>
> MAX LUCADO

able! It was a helicopter. Darin saw it first. As it got nearer to us, it slowed, and then began descending toward the valley about a half mile from the plane. "They're landing! They've found us," shouted one of the boys. How can I describe the joy that pulsed through each one of us as we began to shout and scream? Our wait was over! The big chopper flew off again, and we realized that they hadn't come for us.

How can I explain the devastation we felt? All we had been holding out for, hoping for, had been cruelly snatched away. We all broke into tears and sobbed, and finally, after about an hour, after the tears had stopped, Arne pulled out his Bible and we read some more. How real it became to us as we read the psalms: "O Lord, my God, I cry by day and Thou dost not answer, and by night but find no rest. Yet in Thee our fathers trusted. They trusted and Thou didst deliver them." So we must continue to trust.

And they did continue to trust. The next day the helicopter returned; this time it came for them. "Over here! Over here!" they hollered. "O God, thank you! You never did forget us. God, we've been here for five days. You never left us, you never did! And I know you never will."

Sometimes we are isolated by the problems of life. Instead of a plane crash, the crash is a marriage or a business or a child. What do we do, and to whom do we turn, when there is no one left to encourage us?

There's a story in the Old Testament about a man who found himself in this very situation. As we examine what steps David took, we prepare ourselves for the time when we have to encourage ourselves.

HATED AND HUNTED

Saul considered David his bitter enemy. He hated him. He hunted him. David fled to escape Saul's jealous wrath. As the young giant-killer's life became more and more like the adventures of The Fugitive, he gathered around him a band of rag-tag warriors who were the off-scouring of Israel. The Bible describes them as, "Everyone who was in distress, everyone who was in debt, and everyone who was discontented" (1 Samuel 22:2). What a group.

Eventually David and his new "army" fled across Israel's border into Philistia, hoping to find safety among the Philistines. They thought Saul would never look for them there.

Now it happened, when David and his men came to Ziklag, on the third day, that the Amalekites had invaded the South and Ziklag, attacked Ziklag and burned it with fire, and had taken captive the women and those who were there, from small to great; they did not kill anyone, but carried them away and went their way. So David and his men came to the city, and there it was, burned with fire; and their wives, their sons, and their daughters had been taken captive. Then, David and the people who were with him lifted up their voices and wept, until they had no more power to weep. And David's two wives, Ahinoam the Jezreelitess, and Abigail the widow of Nabal the Carmelite, had been taken captive. Now David was greatly distressed, for the people spoke of stoning him, because the soul of all the people was grieved, every man for his sons and his daughters (1 Samuel 30:1–6).

As the initial wave of grief subsided, David's men began to point their fingers at him. They believed if it hadn't been for David, they would not be going through this experience. They talked of stoning and killing him.

I can't imagine anything more stressful, more frightening, more discouraging, more "why don't I just give up?" than this moment in David's life. All human support systems had vanished. Those who were nearest to him had turned against him. David was left alone to experience his grief and to wrestle with the questions that surely must have filled his mind.

A YOUNG MAN'S SECRET

"But David strengthened himself in the Lord his God" comments 1 Samuel 30:6. In his moment of distress, in the heat of discouragement, the young king turned to the one true God, *his* God, for encouragement. There was nowhere else to go. Life had reduced his options to one. Sooner or later, life does that to all of us.

As a pastor (the only one in the church who doesn't have a pastor), I've had to learn how to encourage myself. I have discovered that our loving Father has provided all the resources we need. It is true that we are commanded to bear one another's burdens and encourage one another and edify and lift one another up, but there will be times when no one will be there for us but God. In those crucial moments we, like David, need to encourage ourselves in the Lord our God.

David's aloneness may have been his first step toward wholeness. There can be great healing in solitude. But let's be honest. Silence and solitude don't seem to have a place in today's world. Jean Fleming, in her book *Finding Focus in a Whirlwind World,* makes this observation:

> We live in a noisy, busy world. Silence and solitude are not twentieth-century words. They fit the era of Victorian lace and high button shoes and kerosene lamps better than the age of television, video arcades, and joggers wired with earphones. We have become a people with an aversion to quiet and an uneasiness with being alone.[1]

Jim Elliott, the martyred missionary, once wrote in his journal: "I think the devil has made it his business to monopolize on three elements: noise, hurry, and crowds. Satan is quite aware of the power of silence."[2]

It's not difficult to find examples in the Bible of people who, because of isolation, needed encouragement. God put Moses on the back side of a desert for forty years before He sent him to lead the exodus. God withdrew Elijah to a cave in Mount Horeb so that he could hear the still, small voice of God. Jesus, too, often withdrew to the seashore or the mountains to be alone with the Father.

There is ministry in solitude—to be alone, to be quiet, so you can talk to God and God can talk to you. David knew that. His psalms show us that he understood the importance of getting alone with God, whether it be in a cave or on a mountainside.

TOOLS FOR SOLITUDE

If a man considers his time to be so valuable that he cannot find time to keep quiet and be alone, that man will eventually be of no value to anyone. To spend all of one's time with people, is to soon have nothing to give to any of them.

Susanna Wesley, the mother of John and Charles Wesley, had nineteen children. She was committed to solitude. In the middle of her busy day, she would pull her apron up over her head and have her quiet time. When the apron went up, the children knew mom was praying and reading her Bible and they left her alone.

> *"I am always hopeful, for a Christian is a prisoner of hope."*
> BISHOP DESMOND TUTU

There are times when the only way to find the encouragement we need is to get alone. Believe me, it can be a very enriching experience. But how can we make the most of it? I believe God has given us at least two tools for making solitude work for us.

1. The tool of Scripture

David was well acquainted with the Old Testament and often turned to it for help and encouragement. It was David who wrote these words about the Scriptures as he knew them:

> The statutes of the Lord are right, rejoicing the heart.... More to be desired are they than gold...sweeter also than honey and the honeycomb. Moreover by them Your servant is warned, and in keeping them there is great reward (Psalm 19:8, 10, 11).

Unless your law had been my delight, I would then have perished in my affliction (Psalm 119:92).

In the previous chapter, I mentioned Romans 15:4—"For whatever things were written before were written for our learning, that we through the patience and comfort [encouragement] of the Scriptures might have hope." Are you familiar with the encouragement of the Scriptures?

The LORD is my light and my salvation: whom shall I fear? (Psalm 27:1).

I sought the LORD, and He heard me, and delivered me from all my fears (Psalm 34:4).

Oh, taste and see that the LORD is good; blessed is the man who trusts in Him! (Psalm 34:8).

Why are you cast down, O my soul? And why are you disquieted within me? Hope in God; for I shall yet praise Him, the help of my countenance and my God (Psalm 43:5).

God is our refuge and strength, a very present help in trouble. Therefore we will not fear, even though the earth be removed, and though the mountains be carried into the midst of the sea; though its waters roar and be troubled, though the mountains shake with its swelling (Psalm 46:1–3).

Be still, and know that I am God; I will be exalted among the nations, I will be exalted in the earth! The Lord of hosts is with us; the God of Jacob is our refuge (Psalm 46:10–11).

When you are discouraged, the best friend you have apart from your personal prayer relationship with God is His Word.

2. The tool of song

David also used song to lift his spirit during the discouraging times of life. He was a great musician and poet; his Psalms are actually praise hymns to God. Yet he was by no means alone in his use of song to counteract discouragement.

Habakkuk prophesied during a period of history when Israel was quite wicked. Habakkuk asked God to judge the sin of His people and God obliged. But the prophet was astonished that God chose the Chaldeans to inflict this judgment. The Chaldeans (or Babylonians) were much more wicked than the Israelites. Habakkuk couldn't understand why God would use a nation more evil than Israel to chasten His people. At the end of the brief book that bears his name, Habakkuk puts the intense conflict aside and worships his God in song. Some scholars think Habakkuk was a Levite responsible for leading the temple choir. Listen to his song of worship to a sovereign God.

> Though the fig tree may not blossom, nor fruit be on the vines; though the labor of the olive may fail, and the fields yield no food; though the flock may be cut off from the fold, and there be no herd in the stalls—Yet I will rejoice in the Lord, I will joy in the God of my salvation (Habakkuk 3:17–18).

G. Campbell Morgan, a conservative expositor of the Word from the last generation, surprised me when he wrote about Habakkuk's song:

> I hope I shall produce no shock when I translate verse 18 literally. Take the first Hebrew word [of verse 18] and express it quite literally, and this is it: "I will jump for joy in the Lord." Take the second of the words and translate it

with equal literalness and this is it: "I will spin around in the God of my salvation."[3]

In a moment of deep discouragement, Habakkuk used music to lift himself up, even to the point where he said, "I am ready to jump for joy to the God of my salvation, and spin around because of who God is."

Over the years, God has used music again and again to minister to my heart, to encourage me. Once when my wife was seriously ill and the doctors could not find the cause of her illness, someone gave me a tape of Andre Crouch's great chorus, "Through it all, I've learned to trust in Jesus, I've learned to trust in God." I played that song over and over until I wore out the tape.

Music is one of God's most blessed gifts and you can encourage yourself through song. Here are two more of my favorite, encouraging songs.

Great is Thy faithfulness, O God my Father!
There is no shadow of turning with Thee;
Thou changest not, Thy compassions, they fail not:
As Thou hast been, Thou forever wilt be.
from *Great Is Thy Faithfulness*
When peace, like a river, attendeth my way,
When sorrows like sea billows roll—
Whatever my lot, Thou hast taught me to say,
It is well, it is well with my soul.
from *It Is Well with My Soul*

A MODERN-DAY DAVID

Billy Graham burst onto the scene of American religion in 1949. He was a young, unknown preacher who began to gather crowds wherever he spoke. He came to Los Angeles, received much press, and eventually became a household word and a nationally-known evangelist.

But before Billy Graham was so well-known, another young man rose to the top in the American religious scene. His name was Chuck Templeton. Chuck Templeton started out as a strong, conservative evangelist. Somewhere along the way, however, he was influenced by liberals. They eroded his confidence in the Scriptures and he came to believe the Bible was not God's Word. Chuck was a friend of Billy Graham's. On one occasion he said to Dr. Graham, "Bill, you cannot refuse to think. To do that is to die intellectually. Not to think is to sin against your Creator. You can't stop thinking. That's intellectual suicide."

Templeton's charge stung, and Graham continued to wrestle with both conscience and intellect. The resolution came at a student conference at Forest Home, a retreat in the San Bernardino Mountains near Los Angeles. Both Graham and Templeton were featured speakers, and their conversations, joined by others asking similar questions, rekindled Billy's doubts. In fresh turmoil, he went for a walk in the serene pine forest. About fifty yards off a main trail, he sat for a long time on a large rock, his Bible spread open on a tree stump. As he struggled once more with his doubts and his commitment, he finally made the pragmatic decision to abandon doubt and cling to commitment. With a spirit of surrender he said, "Oh, God, I cannot prove certain things. I cannot answer some of the questions Chuck is raising and some of the other people are raising. But I accept this Book by faith as the Word of God." He later explained: "I could not live without facing my doubts."[4]

Graham's conscious resolution that he would never again entertain any doubts about the authority of Scripture galvanized his faith and, as he later observed, "gave power and authority to my preaching that has never left me. The gospel in my hands became a hammer and a flame.... I felt as though I had a rapier in my hands and that the power of the Bible was slashing deeply into men's consciousness, leading them to surrender to God."[5]

I want to ask you one simple question: who is Chuck Templeton? Most of us don't know, because we have forgotten him. But Billy Graham will always be remembered. Why? Because in a moment alone with God and His Word, he encouraged himself in the Lord. And God prepared him to be the man all of us have come to admire for his faithful preaching of the gospel of Jesus Christ.

ENCOURAGING YOURSELF

Life can often make us feel as if we're living in the cabin of a small plane that has crashed in the mountains. We are surrounded by snow and overwhelmed by the rocks which tower over us. It seems as if no one cares. No one comes to our rescue. We are left alone, abandoned in the prison of our own personal problems. There is no way out and there can be no way in for any helper.

When this moment comes, remember the secret of a wise young man who would become king: "David strengthened himself in the Lord his God" (1 Samuel 30:6).

LOVE IN ACTION

The following story by J. Oswald Sanders demonstrates how God can communicate His strength and encouragement to a discouraged individual.

While I was general director of the Overseas Missionary Fellowship, on one occasion I was to go to a conference of our missionaries in one of our fields. It was a Muslim field, a terribly resistant area where there had been no previous missionary work at all. They were starting right at the very bedrock, against tremendous opposition, and had seen practically no fruit.

The night before I was to go to them, I went to sleep late with this burden on my heart. I woke up in the night and prayed, "Lord, you must give me a message." Half asleep, I picked up a copy of the New Testament by C. K. Williams, a British translator. My wife had been reading through and marking it. It came open at 2 Corinthians chapters 4 and 5 where she had underlined four statements: "We do not lose heart" (4:1); and again, "We do not lose heart" (4:16); "We are of good courage always" (5:6); and, "We are of good courage" (5:8).

Immediately I knew that here was the Lord's message. I was fully awake now, and the Lord brought ideas from the passage quickly to my mind. It was undoubtedly His word for us then, and I trust it will be His word to you as well—for I believe it has relevance to people in every day and every age.

Why should we never lose heart? Because through God's mercy we have been entrusted with a ministry, the ministry of the new covenant. Because we are endowed every day with new strength, as we learn to appropriate it. Because we have been given the Holy Spirit, part-payment and promise of more. Because we are engrossed and enraptured with the eternal. And because we know that at the proper time there will be an assured harvest.

Therefore, we do not lose heart![6]

FRIEND THERAPY

FRIEND THERAPY

Some time ago, the following letter from an airline pilot appeared in Ann Landers' column in our local newspaper.

In August of 1991, I was told I had brain cancer, and my chances of living another five years were, at best, 50-50. When word of this leaked out to my friends, two of them began a letter-and-card-writing campaign, and all the pilots employed by our airline got involved.

The response was overwhelming. I received stacks of cards and letters every day. My doctors and nurses also let me know that they were interested in my recovery, gave me a lot of tender, loving care, and the treatment that I received from the radiation department where I took my radiation was incredible. And the all-female team in that department deserves special mention for its perpetual smiles and supportive attitude.

My pilot buddies collected enough money to send me and my whole family to Disney World for a beautiful vacation. Surrounded by all that love, I couldn't help but get better. I am now classified as a cancer survivor, and the support of my friends continues to this very day. I am convinced that friend therapy can be a big factor in recovery.

"Friend therapy." I had never heard the term before. But what better way to describe encouragement? Remember our dictionary definition of encouragement: "The act of inspiring others with renewed courage, a renewed spirit, or renewed hope." That's what this pilot experienced. People came alongside him during a difficult time to give him renewed courage, a renewed spirit, and renewed hope. That's encouragement; that's friend therapy.

THE "ONE ANOTHERNESS" OF THE CHRISTIAN FAITH

God has called His people to practice friend therapy. The New Testament tells us to instruct and teach one another, admonish one another, stimulate one another, build up one another, pray for one another, carry burdens for one another, confess our sins to one another, submit to one another, help one another physically and materially, and encourage one another. These commands have been given to all of us, not just to pastors and church leaders. We are all called to practice the "one anotherness" of the Christian faith. The Book of Ecclesiastes explains why:

> Two are better than one.... For if they fall, one will lift up
> his companion. But woe to him who is alone when he falls,
> for he has no one to help him up (Ecclesiastes 4:9, 10).

We need one another for encouragement. I was forcefully reminded of that one summer not too long ago.

For the past several years I have set aside one week of conference time to minister the Word of God at a beautiful conference center near Fresno, California. We Californians refer to the place simply as "Hume Lake."

I've had some pretty unique experiences at Hume which do not fall under the heading of preaching the Word. Most of these adventures involve my relationship with motorcycles. I've crashed so many times that nowadays it takes me until Thursday or Friday of the conference week to generate enough courage to climb on one of those things.

Last year I went to Hume Lake by myself. My wife wasn't there to read me the riot act if I so much as thought of riding a motorcycle, so you guessed it! On Wednesday I jumped on a Honda 250 and headed to the mountains to see God's beautiful handiwork.

Now, I need to tell you that I have never gotten much of a kick out of riding on the beaten paths. The real advantage of a motorcycle is that it can take you where nothing else can go.

So on this day, I headed out for the uncharted, seldom-traveled sections of the Cleveland National Forest. Soon I was above the timberline where the air seems so clean and the sky looks so blue.

I don't know exactly when I realized that I didn't know where I was. But I distinctly remember thinking that I did not know which way to turn in order to head back home.

The motorcycle I was riding hadn't been used in some time and the gas mixture didn't seem quite right. So while I was trying to decide which direction pointed toward home, I was also fiddling with the choke, trying to get the engine to run a little smoother.

> "The best proof that Christ has risen is that he is still alive. And for...our contemporaries, the only way of seeing him alive is for us Christians to love one another."
>
> LOUIS EVELY

All at once, I hit a ditch that crossed the path on which I was riding. Almost before I knew it, I laid the Honda down on its side.

Although the accident really scared me, I did not seem to be hurt. So I picked the bike up, climbed on, and kicked the starter. The engine responded and I started off down the path toward I-don't-know-where.

Just then I looked down at my foot and realized that one of my socks was turning red. I had opened a gash on my leg (which later took seventeen stitches to close).

Now I was really frightened. *What if I really am lost? What if I can't find my way back to the conference center? What if I can't stop the bleeding? My word—I'm going to die at Hume Lake.*

At that moment, I felt fear creeping into my spirit. I didn't know where I was. I didn't know how to get back to where I needed to be. I didn't know how seriously I had cut my leg. And I was foolish enough to be alone. No one was there to help me.

I've replayed this incident in my mind many times. I think my experience in the mountains at Hume Lake is a micropicture of the way life is for many people—lost in the scheme of things, unsure which way to turn, hurt and unaware of it. Most of all, they are alone; no one is around to help lessen the fear.

Solomon was right. When we fall down, we need someone who can help us back up. We desperately need the ministry of encouragement.

THE MINISTRY OF ENCOURAGEMENT

This ministry of encouragement stands near the top of God's priority list. At least fifteen passages in the New Testament talk about "one-another" ministry. Five of them deal with encouragement:

So comfort and encourage each other with this news (1 Thessalonians 4:18, TLB).

So encourage each other to build each other up, just as you are already doing (1 Thessalonians 5:11, TLB).

Now we exhort you, brethren, warn those who are unruly, comfort [encourage] the fainthearted, uphold the weak, be patient with all (1 Thessalonians 5:14).

But exhort [encourage] one another daily, while it is called "Today," lest any of you be hardened through the deceitfulness of sin (Hebrews 3:13).

Not forsaking the assembling of ourselves together, as is the manner of some, but exhorting [encouraging] one another, and so much the more as you see the Day approaching (Hebrews 10:25).

These passages challenge us to a ministry of concern for one another. These are not instructions for a pastor to encourage his flock, as important as that may be. This is not a vocational command. These words are found in the job description of every believer.

Probably the best definition I've heard for encouragement is "Pouring courage into somebody who needs it." God knows we don't have to look far to see people in need. To understand how we can encourage one another, it's helpful to know what it takes to be encouraged. What encourages you? What things pour courage into your own soul?

WHAT WE SENSE

Eliphaz, Bildad, and Zophar were three friends who came to encourage Job in his time of deep despair. While these men didn't end up being much of an encouragement to Job, initially they did one thing right—they came alongside him. They sat with him on the ash heap for seven days in silence. They didn't say a word. Job must have sensed these men really cared about him. That's how it usually is with encouragement; you can sense it. Usually it occurs when people give us what I call focused attention.

Do you remember the story of Mary and Martha in the New Testament? It's a study in focused attention. Martha was like so many of us. She couldn't believe the Lord Jesus had really come to her house. She was out in the kitchen trying to make everything just right for the important person who was visiting her home. But Mary, her sister, employed a different method of honoring Christ. Mary sat at His feet and focused all her attention on Him. And the Lord said it was Mary who did the better thing.

Do you know what it's like when people focus their attention on you? Focused attention lets you know people really care. It lets you know they're not concerned about anything or anyone else for the moment. They are there just for you. Focused attention feels good and it's so encouraging.

WHAT WE HEAR

I can also be encouraged by what I hear. If I sense someone genuinely cares about me, that person's words can be powerful. As the adage goes, "Nobody cares how much you know until they know how much you care." People sometimes open their mouths first, before they've earned the right. But if they've earned the right with a little focused attention, then we can be encouraged by what they say and by what we hear.

The Book of Proverbs speaks often about encouragement. Here's one example: "Anxious hearts are very heavy but a word of encouragement does wonders!" (Proverbs 12:25, TLB) Have you ever been weighed down by anxiety when someone came along and spoke a good word which lifted your spirit? During one of the deepest, darkest times in my life, a fellow pastor called me just to say, "David, I want you to know I love you, and I know you are going through some hurt. I want you to know I'm

> "He climbs highest who helps another up."
>
> ZIG ZIGLAR

here if you need me. I want to pray with you." And he prayed with me on the phone. He called me every week for several weeks with a word of encouragement. He poured courage into my heart.

During World War II, after Hitler blasted his way across France demanding the unconditional surrender of the Allied Forces in the European theater, thousands of British and French troops dug in along the coast of Northern France in a final effort to hold off the German forces. Trapped on the beaches of Dunkirk, they knew they would soon be obliterated. But during that agonizing period, they broadcast a terse message across the English Channel consisting of just three words: "And if not...." Was it a code? No. It was a reference to the Old Testament story of Shadrach, Meshach, and Abednego. As these three men stood before King Nebuchadnezzar and his fiery furnace, they said, "Our God whom we serve is able to deliver us from the burning fiery furnace, and He will deliver us from your hand, O king. But if not, let it be known to you, O king, that we do not serve your gods, nor will we worship the gold image which you have set up" (Daniel 3:17, 18).

When the English soldiers back home heard those words, they understood them completely. They knew the biblical context and understood what it meant. It was a "shorthand" message of courage designed to help them to stand strong when everything was against them.

WHAT WE READ

I am encouraged not only by what I sense and hear, but by what I read. One of the great tools of encouragement is what you write to someone. Believe it or not, two or three sentences can turn a person's life around.

When my son David was in the ninth grade, he played on the varsity basketball team. He played his first varsity game at Grossmont High School. About midway through the first quarter, he entered the game. He was wired pretty tightly. That's an intimidating experience for a freshman.

He was so nervous when he took his first shot that he undershot the basket and didn't hit a thing. You know what happens when you do that in an opposing school's gym? They have a little cheer for you: "Aiiirrrr Ball!" Say it loudly. Doesn't that sound great? When you're the one who shot the air ball, you wilt into a little spot on the floor and die.

When David got home that night he was about as discouraged as any young man could be. The next morning I could see he was still down. I wasn't sure what to do. But I remember going to my office and writing him a letter. I tried to think of everything positive I could say to encourage him. I told him he had played a varsity game in a school located in the eighth-largest city in America. I told him what a great career he was going to have. I told him how much I loved him. Then I put the letter in an envelope and had it delivered to him at school.

That night I couldn't wait for him to come home from school. I thought, *He's going to rush right in and tell me how this note changed his life*. Right? Wrong. I had to wait until Father's Day a few months later. At the bottom of his card he wrote, "Thanks for the note of encouragement."

WHAT WE FEEL

We are also encouraged by what we feel from others. I'm talking about touching. Now, don't get the wrong idea; I'm talking about touching with the right motive, the right heart. Have you ever noticed how often in the New Testament Jesus touched people?

> Jesus put forth his hand and touched the leper saying, "I will. Be thou clean." And immediately the leprosy was removed (Luke 5:13).
>
> So He touched her hand, and the fever left her. And she arose and served them (Matthew 8:15).
>
> So Jesus had compassion and touched their eyes. And immediately their eyes received sight, and they followed Him (Matthew 20:34).
>
> He took him aside from the multitude, and put His fingers in his ears, and He spat and touched his tongue.... Immediately his ears were opened, and the impediment of his tongue was loosed (Mark 7:33, 35).

And He touched his ear and healed him (Luke 22:51).

Paul touched people, too. "And it happened that the father of Publius lay sick of a fever and dysentery. Paul went in to him and prayed, and he laid his hands on him and healed him" (Acts 28:8). You may say, "Well, Dr. Jeremiah, I don't have the gift of healing. I'm not Jesus Christ and I'm not Paul, so don't talk to me about touching." Let me tell you something. God put our being into the envelope we call skin, and the skin is the sensory receiver of many of the messages we receive. Something special happens when someone touches us.

Recently in Charlotte, North Carolina, I visited a pastor I hadn't seen for many years. After Donna and I finished eating dinner with him and his wife, we returned to the church where we had left our car. My friend thanked us for taking time to be with them, and we thanked them for the wonderful dinner. Then he wrapped his arms around me and hugged me. He told me he loved me and that he had a new desire to pray for us and our ministry. I can still feel the place where his hands touched my back.

Why are we so afraid to touch? Probably because so often touching is misunderstood. That's unfortunate, but I believe there is a way to touch people that communicates love, warmth, and encouragement (even without reviving the New Testament's "holy kiss"!). Sometimes it's putting your arm around a brother or sister and giving a squeeze. Sometimes it's a hug.

It's wondrous what a hug can do.
A hug can cheer you when you're blue.
A hug can say, "I love you so,"
Or, "I sure hate to see you go."
A hug is, "Welcome back again,"
And "Great to see you! Where've you been?"
A hug can soothe a small child's pain

And bring a rainbow after rain.
The hug—there's no doubt about it—
We scarcely could survive without it!
A hug delights and warms and charms.
It must be why God gave us arms.
Hugs are great for fathers and mother,
Sweet for sisters, swell for brothers.
And chances are your favorite aunts
Love them more than potted plants.
Kittens crave them. Puppies love them.
Heads of state are not above them.
A hug can break the language barrier,
And make your travel so much merrier,
No need to fret about your store of 'em.
The more you give, the more there's more of 'em.
So stretch those arms without delay
And *give someone a hug today!!!*[1]

This simple little poem has a marvelous message: we encourage people when we touch them with the love of God. People are encouraged by what they feel.

ENCOURAGING ONE ANOTHER

The body of Christ is a family whose members are to be mutually involved with one another. One of the one-another ministries God calls us to practice is the ministry of encouragement.

I know that I am encouraged by what I sense, by what I hear, by what I read, and by what I feel. I doubt that I'm much different from you.

LOVE IN ACTION

On the coldest days of the northern winter, we often find that our car battery has lost its charge during the night. The engine will not turn over because the battery is too weak. The ministry of encouragement is like a car that comes alongside ours and gives us a jump start. The strength of the operative car is transferred into the weak battery, and the inoperative car is rejuvenated to action.

When we see people who are discouraged, saddened by the hardships of life, or simply tired of the Christian path of obedience, we need to come alongside and give them a spiritual jump start. As Christ and other members of the Body of Christ strengthen us, we can strengthen others. By God's Holy Spirit, we can assist each other in the Christian life.[2]

MR. ENCOURAGEMENT

MR. ENCOURAGEMENT

Some of the greatest success stories of history have followed a word of encouragement from a loved one or a trusting friend. Had it not been for a confident and encouraging wife, Sophia, we might not have listed among the great names of literature the name of Nathaniel Hawthorne. When Nathaniel, a heartbroken man, went home to tell his wife he was a failure and had been fired from his job in a customhouse, she surprised him with an exclamation of joy.

"Now," she said triumphantly, "you can write your book!"

"Yes," replied the man, with sagging confidence, "and what shall we live on while I am writing it?"

To his amazement, she opened a drawer and pulled out a substantial sum of money.

"Where on earth did you get that?" he exclaimed.

"I have always known you were a man of genius," she told him. "I knew that someday you would write a masterpiece. So every week, out of the money you gave me for housekeeping, I saved a little bit. So here is enough to last us for one whole year."

From her trust and confidence came one of the greatest novels of American literature, *The Scarlet Letter*.[1]

When most people who've achieved great things tell their stories, they mention those who encouraged them along the way. Many of the great musical composers at one time or another were ready to quit, but someone stepped in and said, "No, you can't quit!" Many of the great writers submitted hundreds of manuscripts before they were ever published; they would have given up if someone hadn't come along and said, "No, I believe in you. Keep writing. You can do it." Many great athletes would have given up on themselves, but there was somebody who wouldn't allow it. When these folks tell their stories, they all talk about the person who kept them going, the one who wouldn't let them quit, the one who spoke a word of encouragement at exactly the right moment.

> *Nobody cares how much you know until they know how much you care.*

The New Testament tells of a man who distinguished himself as an encourager, a motivator of others. The man's name was Barnabas and his story is wrapped up in the exciting details that describe the first-century church.

BARNABAS, THE ENCOURAGER

Barnabas was a disciple in the early assembly when, in order to meet the needs of the church, "All who believed were together, and had all things in common, and sold their possessions and goods, and divided them among all, as anyone had need" (Acts 2:44–45).

As a landowner in Cyprus (a productive, fertile city on the border of Syria), we may assume that Barnabas was a wealthy man. We know for sure that he was one of those rare personalities who thinks life consists of helping and encouraging others. In fact, in every place where he shows up in the New Testament record, he is doing just that.

This man was such an incurable motivator that the apostles finally changed his name from Joses (Joseph) to Barnabas, which means "son of encouragement." If he were on the scene today we might call him "Mr. Encouragement."

Barnabas was not just a back-slapping stroker, however; he was a sincere man of God. He is described as "a good man, full of the Holy Spirit and of faith" (Acts 11:24).

Barnabas was good in the sense that he was generous. He was kind. He wasn't passive about his goodness, either; his virtue was active. He proactively involved himself in the lives of others.

It's not overstating it to say that Barnabas was good in the sense that God is good. His goodness came from a special relationship— he was full of the Holy Spirit who controlled him. And Barnabas was filled with faith—faith in God and faithfulness in representing God. That's the kind of man he was: full of the Holy Spirit and full of faith.

If we were to search the Scriptures for the outstanding example of a godly encourager, without question, we would end our search right here with this man: Barnabas.

THREE KEY QUALITIES

As we survey the life of Barnabas, we find three transferable qualities that we can build into our own lives.

1. Performers, not pretenders

The Book of Acts not only tells us that the first-century believers had "all things in common," it also explains that they "sold their possessions and goods, and divided them among all, as anyone had need" (Acts 2:45). It should not surprise us to learn that Barnabas sold some of his expensive real estate and gave the proceeds to the church.

Nor was there anyone among them who lacked; for all who were possessors of lands and houses sold them, and brought the proceeds of the things that were sold, and laid them at the apostles' feet; and they distributed to each as anyone had need. And Joses, who was also named Barnabas by the apostles (which is translated Son of Encouragement), a Levite of the country of Cyprus, having land, sold it, and brought the money and laid it at the apostles' feet (Acts 4:34–37).

By his act of charity, Barnabas illustrates the first of the three principles: Encouragers *perform* while others *pretend*. The impact of Barnabas's story is probably strengthened by its placement right next to the story of Ananias and Sapphira. This couple also made a gift to the church. It is the contrast between these two "acts of love" that forms the basis for our principle, Encouragers perform while others pretend.

When word of Barnabas's generosity spread through the early church family, there must have been much rejoicing and gratitude. Perhaps his gift was the catalyst that prompted others to give, including Ananias. We know that Barnabas's and Ananias's gifts were related. The connective at the beginning of Acts 5 makes that clear.

But here's the catch: Barnabas performed while Ananias pretended. When Barnabas gave his gift, he gave it all, keeping back nothing for himself. His gift was genuine, sincere, without hypocrisy.

Ananias and his wife also sold some property, but that's where the similarities ended:

But a certain man named Ananias, with Sapphira his wife, sold a possession. And he kept back part of the proceeds, his wife also being aware of it, and brought a certain part and laid it at the apostle's feet (Acts 5:1–2).

These two were like many would-be encouragers today. They

wanted the recognition but didn't like the requirements. They just couldn't bring themselves to make the full sacrifice, as Barnabas had done. But because they wanted the same level of applause, they pretended to give it all and kept back some for themselves. Their "act of love" was not genuine. It was tarnished with deceit and self-ishness. That's the reason they were judged so harshly—they gave under false pretenses (Peter called it "lying" to the Holy Spirit, v. 3). They missed the blessing that could have been theirs, because they were unwilling to pay the price up front. They pretended!

If we think back over our own lives, most of us are able to remember when we have been at the other end of Ananias-style encouragement. Oh, the words were said; but somehow we sensed they were just the well-rehearsed speeches expected at such times. The deed was done, but the doer couldn't hide the twinge of resent-ment that transformed his "act of love" into an act of begrudging duty.

Some of my friends tell me that caring for their aging parents sometimes brings this struggle to the surface. And if we are not careful, those of us who serve others in the ministry can fall into the habit of "professional" encouragement—helping people solely out of a sense of obligation. Let us learn well the lesson of Barnabas and Ananias. True encouragers do not pretend, they perform.

2. Potential, not problems

Barnabas is next mentioned in the New Testament in connec-tion with the apostle Paul's rise to prominence within the church. The story begins with the conversion of Paul on the road to Damascus. The bright light, the voice from heaven, the fall to the ground, all combined with the genuine work of the Holy Spirit in Paul's heart to totally transform him.

After this miraculous event, instead of persecuting the followers of Christ, Paul desires to join them. "And when Saul had come to

Jerusalem [after his conversion], he tried to join the disciples" (Acts 9:26). Unless we understand Paul's history up to this point in his life, we might not be able to appreciate the rest of Acts 9:26: "But they [the disciples] were all afraid of him, and did not believe that he was a disciple."

To refresh your memory, here's what Paul was before his dramatic experience with God on the Damascus road:

> As for Saul, he made havoc of the church, entering every house, and dragging off men and women, committing them to prison (Acts 8:3).
>
> Then Saul, still breathing threats and murder against the disciples of the Lord, went to the high priest and asked letters from him to the synagogues of Damascus, so that if he found any who were of the Way [Christians], whether men or women, he might bring them bound to Jerusalem (Acts 9:1–2).

It's not hard to see why the true followers of Christ were skeptical of Paul's supposed conversion! And to bring him right into the center of their fellowship? Unthinkable! To everyone, that was, except Barnabas. Barnabas had heard Paul's testimony, perhaps first-hand. Barnabas believed Paul and was willing to stick his neck out for him.

> But Barnabas took him and brought him to the apostles. And he declared to them how he had seen the Lord on the road, and that He had spoken to him, and how he had preached boldly at Damascus in the name of Jesus. So he was with them at Jerusalem, coming in and going out (Acts 9:27–28).

The second transferable quality of an encourager is this: Encouragers see potential where others see problems. When no one wanted anything to do with Paul, Barnabas stood up with him and for him. He believed in him!

One of the tell-tale signs of a Christian who has the gift of encouragement is to be found right here. He champions the underdog. He'll jump on the bandwagon when everyone else is jumping off. If, at the zenith of his influence as an apostle, Paul had been asked to name his number one encourager, he would have spoken of the Holy Spirit and he would have mentioned Barnabas.

One other incident in the life of Barnabas reveals this same pattern. The Jerusalem church had commissioned Paul and Barnabas to carry a letter of affirmation to the Gentile Christians in Antioch (see Acts 15:22–29). After delivering the letter, the two men stayed on in Antioch for a short time "teaching and preaching the word of the Lord" (Acts 15:35). Apparently Paul felt it was time to leave Antioch and suggested they backtrack and visit every church where they had previously presented the gospel.

> *"How many people stop because so few say, 'Go'?"*
>
> CHARLES R. SWINDOLL

Then after some days Paul said to Barnabas, "Let us now go back and visit our brethren in every city where we have preached the word of the Lord, and see how they are doing." Now Barnabas was determined to take with them John called Mark. But Paul insisted that they should not take with them the one who had departed from them in Pamphylia, and had not gone with them to the work. Then the contention became so sharp that they parted from one another. And so Barnabas took Mark and sailed to Cyprus; but Paul chose Silas and departed being commended by the brethren to the grace of God (Acts 15:36–40).

Young John Mark was the source of a strong disagreement between Paul and Barnabas. As far as Paul was concerned, John Mark had disqualified himself by deserting Paul during the first missionary journey (Acts 13:5, 13). But Barnabas didn't focus on

Mark's problems; he saw his potential. Barnabas believed in John Mark so deeply that he parted company with Paul in order to take John Mark! Encouragers see potential where others see problems.

And here's one additional observation: Isn't it interesting that the one who earlier in his life needed someone to believe in him was, later in his life, unwilling to believe in another? To Paul's credit, he did eventually change his mind about this young man. At the close of his second letter to Timothy, Paul writes: "Get Mark and bring him with you, for he is useful to me for ministry" (2 Timothy 4:11).

One of the greatest tools any leader has in his tool box is the tool of encouragement. In the book *Raising Self-Reliant Children in a Self-Indulging World,* H. Stephen Glenn and Jane Nelsen make this point emphatically:

Children feel encouraged when we see them as assets rather than objects, see mistakes as opportunities to learn rather than as failures, and invite participation and contributions rather than directing and demanding compliance.

Jonas Salk, the great scientist and the discoverer of the vaccine against polio, understood the concept of being encouraging. He was once asked, "How does this outstanding achievement, which has effectively brought an end to the word *polio* in our vocabulary, cause you to view your previous 200 failures?"

His response (paraphrased) was, "I never had 200 failures in my life. My family didn't think in terms of failure. They taught in terms of experiences and what could be learned. I just made my 201st discovery. I couldn't have made it without learning from the previous 200 experiences."

Winston Churchill, too, was raised with encouragement. He was not intimidated by errors. When he made one, he simply thought the problem through again. Someone asked him, "Sir Winston, what in your school experience best prepared you to lead Britain out of her darkest hour?"

Winston thought a minute and then said, "It was the two years I spent at the same level in high school."

"Did you fail?"

"No," replied Winston. "I had two opportunities to get it right." What Britain needed was not brilliance, but perseverance when things were going badly.

When we encourage children and invite them to explore possibilities, we help them develop positive attitudes toward learning from experience and even from seeming failures.[2]

I know about this principle from personal experience. In college I took a speech class for one simple reason: There was a young lady in the class I had my eye on. (Her name was Donna Thompson. I would later change it.) She was a good student, I was a goof-off—a royal goof-off! One day, our professor, John Reed, took me aside and said, "David, I don't know what other people have said to you, but you have potential and I believe in you. You shouldn't mess around. You ought to take your potential seriously. Someday you might even be a preacher." I laughed at his words, but I never forgot what he said. Even though it happened many years ago, I remember that moment as if it happened yesterday.

Isn't it interesting that we don't forget those moments when someone says an encouraging word which turns us around and heads us in the right direction? I wonder: Who in your sphere of influence could use such an encouraging word?

3. People, not prominence

The third "Barnabas principle" for encouragers is illustrated in the eleventh chapter of Acts. Barnabas had been commissioned by the church in Jerusalem to go as her representative to the Gentile church in Antioch. A great movement of the Spirit had taken hold of that assembly and word about it had reached the leaders in Jerusalem. When Barnabas arrived in Antioch, he did the one thing he always seemed to do in every situation:

> When he came and had seen the grace of God, he was glad, and *encouraged them all* that with purpose of heart they should continue with the Lord (Acts 11:23, emphasis mine).

When he came back to this same church later, he was still on the same page:

> Strengthening the souls of the disciples, exhorting them to continue in the faith, and saying, "We must through many tribulations enter the kingdom of God" (Acts 14:22).

Barnabas's encouragement fanned the flame that was already burning brightly, and "a great many people were added to the Lord" (Acts 11:24). As I read the record of this revival, I can almost feel the excitement in the air. Several times, during my years of ministry, I have sensed that extra-special outpouring of the Spirit. It is something you never forget!

But here's where Barnabas parts company with many evangelists. Instead of climbing up on the platform of this successful campaign, he went to Tarsus to see if he could locate Paul.

> And when he had found him, he brought him to Antioch. So it was that for a whole year they assembled with the church and taught a great many people (Acts 11:26).

More important to Barnabas than any notoriety he might receive was the welfare of the people who were coming to know the Lord in vast numbers. Realizing that alone he was not adequate to the task of teaching and discipleship, Barnabas brought Paul into the center of the revitalized church and shared the teaching ministry with him. Foremost in Barnabas's mind was the growth of these new believers. He wanted them to have the best possible instructor. That's the heart of an encourager! Encouragers care more about people than prominence.

The modern-day Barnabas is far more comfortable behind the scenes, working one-on-one, than in the spotlight of attention. Some of the great encouragers I have known absolutely refuse to be publicly recognized. They are not motivated by anything other than their love for people.

There is one interesting footnote to the Antioch episode in Barnabas's life. Until this time, Barnabas had been in the lead position. The references to the two men always read, "Barnabas and Paul." But from this moment on (with but one exception, Acts 14:14), the order is reversed. Now it is "Paul and Barnabas." I'm sure that suited Barnabas just fine!

One of the great encouragers of our generation is a man by the name of Bob Pierce. It was his compassion for the hurting and hungry people of the world that motivated him to start the ministry of World Vision.

Shortly before his death (of leukemia), Bob had the opportunity to fulfill one of his deepest desires. A man who had been called as a missionary under Pierce's ministry was serving the Lord in Indonesia. His name, too, was Bob—Bob Williams. He had acquired the nickname "Borneo Bob" because of his great love for the people of that region.

Even though he was very ill, Bob Pierce went to Indonesia one last time to see Borneo Bob. When he arrived, Borneo Bob took him around and showed him what God was doing through the various missionary outreaches which had been partially financed by World Vision. As they were going through some of the villages, they came to a river. As they approached the river, they noticed a girl lying on a bamboo mat. Bob Pierce asked Borneo Bob what she was doing there. Borneo Bob explained that she was dying from cancer and had just a few days to live.

The news filled Bob Pierce with anger—not at anyone in particular, just anger at the situation. He asked Borneo Bob, "Why is this girl lying down here in the mud when she should be up in the clinic with somebody to take care of her?" Borneo Bob explained that the girl was from the jungle and preferred to be near the river where it was cooler. She had asked to be put there. So Bob Pierce, the consummate encourager, went over and got down on his knees in the mud. He took the girl's hand and began to stroke it. He prayed for her. She didn't understand anything he said, but after he prayed, she looked up and said something to him. Bob Pierce turned to Borneo Bob and asked, "What did she say?"

He replied, "She just said, 'If I could only sleep again, if I could only sleep again.'" Her cancer was so painful she couldn't sleep. Bob Pierce began to cry. He reached into his pocket, took out his bottle of sleeping pills, and gave them to Borneo Bob, instructing him, "You make sure this young lady gets a good night's sleep as long as these pills last."

Dr. Bob Pierce was ten days from Singapore, the closest place he could get his medication refilled. His gift meant he would go ten nights without any sleep; without those pills, the pain from his own leukemia would keep him wide awake.

No matter how much it hurts, encouragers find a way. I didn't know Bob Pierce personally, but I can't help thinking that every night during those ten days, as he lay awake in pain, he thanked God for the privilege of sacrificially encouraging another human being who didn't even speak his language. Bob and Barnabas were of a kindred spirit!

A NEEDED POPULATION EXPLOSION

Encouragers are a different breed.
They don't pretend…they perform.

They see potential where others see problems.
They care more about people than prominence.
May their tribe increase!

LOVE IN ACTION

When Anne Morrow met Charles Lindbergh, he was a national hero. He had won $40,000 for flying solo across the Atlantic and was flying from city to city promoting aviation. Anne's father was ambassador to Mexico. During Lindbergh's visit to Mexico for the State Department, a love began to grow between the two young people which was to bind them together for forty-seven years. Anne was like her husband, shy and retiring. But despite tragedies in their lives and despite being married to a man always in the lime-light, she went on to become one of America's most popular authors.

In describing their marriage, she gives a clue to the success of her own career. Her husband believed in her to an extraordinary degree. She says:

> To be deeply in love is, of course, a great liberating force and the most common experience that frees.... Ideally, both members of a couple in love free each other to new and different worlds. I was no exception to the general rule. The sheer fact of finding myself loved was unbelievable and changed my world, my feelings about life and myself. I was given confidence, strength, and almost a new character. The man I was to marry believed in me and what I could do, and consequently I found I could do more than I realized.[3]

THE ENCOURAGEMENT ZONE

THE ENCOURAGEMENT ZONE

Their wedding picture mocked them from the table, these two whose minds no longer touched each other. They lived with such a heavy barricade between them that neither battering ram, nor words, nor artilleries of touch could break it down. Somewhere between the oldest child's first tooth and the youngest daughter's graduation they lost each other. Throughout the years, each slowly unraveled that tangled ball of string called self, and as they tugged at stubborn knots, each hid his searching from the other.

Sometimes she cried at night and begged the whispering darkness to tell her who she was. He lay beside her, snoring like a hibernating bear, unaware of her winter.

Once after they had made love, he wanted to tell her how afraid he was of dying, but fearing to show his naked soul, he spoke only of her beauty.

She took a course in modern art, trying to find herself in colors splashed upon a canvas, complaining to other women about men who are insensitive.

He climbed into a tomb called "The Office," wrapped

his mind in a shroud of papers, and buried himself in cus-
tomers.

And slowly the wall between them rose, cemented by
the mortar of indifference. One day, reaching out to touch
each other, they found a barrier they could not penetrate.
Recoiling from the coldness of the stone, each retreated
from the stranger on the other side.

For when love dies, it is not in a moment of angry
battle, nor when fiery bodies lose their heat. But it lies pant-
ing and exhausted, expiring at the bottom of a carefully built
wall it cannot scale.[1]

If you have done any counseling at all, you are nodding your
head in understanding. You know the story; it is all too familiar.
Some marriages that start out strong, end up gasping for air and
dying a slow, painful death. By the time the couple realizes how bad
things are, they have already passed the point of no return.

Part of our predicament today is the media-driven expectations
most couples have as they enter into marriage. George Bernard
Shaw summed up the problem when he wrote:

When two people are under the influence of the most vio-
lent, most insane, most delusive and most transient of pas-
sions, they are required to swear that they will remain in
that excited, abnormal, and exhausting condition, continu-
ously until death do them part.[2]

One middle-aged woman described it this way:

We are led to believe that love is passionate eye-locking
gazes, throbbing temples, and rippling muscles. My husband and I can only experience eyelocking gazes if we both
happen to be wearing our eyeglasses at the same time. To

us, throbbing temples warn of possible high blood pressure
and our muscles tend to be more jiggling than rippling.

Don't you just love honest people?

Some years ago, *Christianity Today* published an article titled,
"The Ideal Relationship and Other Myths about Marriage." The
writer, a Reformed Church pastor from New York, wrote:

> I believe marriage is in trouble today because society and
> the church have a faulty view of it—a deified myth of this
> human, delightful, yet flawed institution.
>
> Though fertility gods have been dethroned by the
> advance of Christianity, today's culture seems to be resur-
> recting them in a more palatable form…. Most voices today
> laud a romantic image of marriage as life's ultimate source
> of true joy.
>
> What is the result? A crash. Thousands of crashes….
> Why? Because in reality every marriage faces conflict, mis-
> understanding, smashed fantasies, and bruised egos. Any
> real marriage held up against the yardstick of total joy will
> measure short. And if relationships that are meant to give
> total joy fail, lives are shattered.[3]

"Conflict, misunderstanding, smashed fantasies, and bruised
egos"—not too encouraging, is it? And this is not just a report, this is
reality. In 1960, 37 percent of all first-time marriages failed; by 1990,
chances of a first-time marriage surviving were only 50 percent. The
June 1993 issue of *Psychology Today* reported that 75 percent of all
couples in America will be affected by infidelity.[4] In marriage the natural tendency is toward deterioration, not improvement. And the
only way marriage partners can offset the process of decay is by taking a proactive approach toward improving their relationship. Both
husband and wife need to master the art of encouragement.

WE REALLY DO NEED EACH OTHER

Perhaps we should begin our discussion by affirming that marriage is from God. It was His idea! It still is! Five times in the creation narrative in Genesis 1, we read that God looked at what He had created and "saw that it was good" (2:9, 12, 18, 21, 25). Then when He had finished with the creation of man, God surveyed His entire work: "Then God saw everything that He had made, and indeed it was very good" (Genesis 1:31). Six times God said that His work in creation was good. No wonder we snap to attention when we read this statement in Genesis 2: "And the LORD God said, 'It is not good that man should be alone; I will make him a helper comparable to him'" (Genesis 2:18).

> "The men who are
> lifting
> the world upward
> and
> onward are those
> who
> encourage more
> than criticize."
>
> ELISABETH HARRISON

It was God's assessment that man should not be alone, that He needed someone to relate to him. So God created woman. Contrary to what some have jokingly said, woman is not a cognate of the words "woe to man." The word "woman" in the Hebrew language is the word *isha*. The word for man is *ish*. Man is *ish,* woman is *isha*. In Genesis 2, we discover how *isha* came to be:

And the LORD God caused a deep sleep to fall on Adam, and he slept; and He took one of his ribs, and closed up the flesh in its place. Then the rib which the LORD God had taken from man He made into a woman, and He brought her to the man. And Adam said: "This is now bone of my bones and flesh of my flesh; she shall be called Woman *[isha],* because she was taken out of Man *[ish]."* Therefore a man shall leave his father and mother and be joined to his wife, and they shall become one flesh. And they were both naked, the man and his wife, and were not ashamed (Genesis 2:21–25).

When God saw that it was not good for the man to be alone, He set out to change things. He caused a great sleep to come upon Adam (the first anesthesia). He took a rib from his side (the first surgery), and out of that rib God fashioned a woman. She was taken from Adam's side, not molded from the ground as was her husband. She was taken from a part of Adam so that Adam was naturally incomplete until they were together. *Ish* could not be complete without *Isha*. St. Augustine put it this way:

If God had meant woman to rule over man, He would have taken her from his head. Had He designed her to be his slave, He would have taken her from his feet. But God took woman out of man's side, for He made her to be a helpmeet and an equal to him.

When God was finished with the creation of Eve, he brought her to Adam and the first wedding took place. When Adam saw Eve, he said, "This is now bone of my bones and flesh of my flesh" (Genesis 2:23). The Living Bible, which I sometimes read for my own personal enjoyment, says that when Adam first saw Eve, he said, "This is it!" There is great excitement in the heart of the first man when he meets the first woman!

Over thirty years ago, in one of the first books on marriage I ever read, I copied this beautiful comment on these words from Genesis 2:

The man is restless while he is missing the rib that was taken out of his side, and the woman is restless until she gets under man's arm, from whence she was taken. It is humbling for the woman to know she was created for the man, but it is to her glory to know that she alone can complete him. Likewise, it is humbling to the man to know that he is incomplete without the woman, but it is to his glory to know that the woman was created for him.[5]

The Old Testament carefully describes how man and woman came into being. Marriage originated with God. When God's blueprint for marriage is followed, it is one of the most wonderful, encouraging experiences one can know while on this earth. We can begin now to create a zone of encouragement at home. Genesis 2 includes some enduring principles which even today can mature, strengthen, and breathe new life into marriages.

A COMMITMENT TO RESPONSIBILITY

For marriages to survive in this decade of divorce, there must be a commitment to responsibility. Unless matrimony is built upon a foundation of mutual dedication, no amount of encouragement will stave off the forces pulling against it. Dr. Robert B. Taylor, author of the book, *Couples: The Art of Staying Together,* wrote, "We're now living in the age of disposability: Use it once, and throw it away. Over the past decade, there has developed a feeling that relationships are equally disposable."[6]

But the Bible knows nothing of throw-away marriages. In the poetic language of the Old Testament, marital responsibility is described in these words: "Therefore, a man shall leave his father and his mother and be joined to his wife, and they shall become one flesh" (Genesis 2:24). There is far more to this statement than first meets the eye:

"Leave" (*asav,* Hebrew) and "join" (*davaq,* Hebrew) are terms associated with covenant treaties. Here, marriage is interpreted as a new relationship bound by mutual oath.

Sexual intimacy is an expression of the union of the two people; however, sexual union by itself is not sufficient to define the biblical concept of marriage.[7]

We have a phrase we use to describe marriage. We call it "tying the knot." I once read a comment from a mountain climber who said that the reason mountain climbers are tied together is to keep the sane ones from going home. Now, there's a thought! One of the reasons God ties the knot in marriage is to keep us from running away when the going gets tough.

Where there is this kind of commitment, the Christian family can truly be an encouragement zone. Ken Canfield thinks this enduring bond between husband and wife affects more than just the two of them:

> The challenge for this generation is to make marriage a prerequisite to fathering. Every day hundreds of children are born without two parents who are committed to building a solid family together. Research confirms that these children are more likely to commit delinquent acts, drop out of school, have children out of wedlock, suffer poverty, receive welfare, and abuse drugs and alcohol. The future is much brighter for children who have two parents in a committed relationship. But the operative word is committed.[8]

For many years Robertson McQuilken was the president of Columbia Bible College. Some years ago he had to resign his position because his wife, Muriel, was suffering the advanced stages of Alzheimer's disease. In March 1990, Robertson announced his resignation in a letter, with these words:

> My dear wife, Muriel, has been in failing mental health for about eight years. So far, I have been able to carry her

ever-growing needs and my leadership responsibilities at CBC. But recently it has become apparent that Muriel is contented most of the time she is with me and almost none of the time I am away from her. It is not just "discontent." She is filled with fear—even terror—that she has lost me and always goes in search of me when I leave home. Then she may be full of anger when she cannot get to me. So it is clear to me that she needs me now full time.

Perhaps it would help you to understand if I shared with you what I shared at the time of the announcement of my resignation in chapel. The decision was made, in a way, 42 years ago when I promised to care for Muriel "in sickness and in health...till death do us part." So, as I told the students and faculty, as a man of my word, integrity has something to do with it. But so does fairness. She has cared for me fully and sacrificially all these years; if I cared for her for the next 40 years I would not be out of debt. Duty, however, can be grim and stoic. But there is more; I love Muriel. She is a delight to me—her childlike dependence and confidence in me, her warm love, occasional flashes of that wit that I used to relish so, her happy spirit and tough resilience in the face of her continually distressing frustration. I do not have to care for her, I get to. It is a high honor to care for so wonderful a person.[9]

When I first read these words I was reminded of the personal example of commitment I have observed in my own family. A few years ago, my mother also died from Alzheimer's disease. I watched my father, who had made a commitment some fifty years earlier, keep his promise to Mom as he stopped everything in his life to minister to her until she was no longer able to live at home.

And then every week he visited her several times, and every time I came to visit, we would go pick up Mom and take her out to dinner. Even when she could not communicate and did not seem to know any of us, Dad went right on loving her and acting as if nothing had changed in their relationship. "Till death do us part" will never be the same to me again!

A COMMITMENT TO INTIMACY

A French historian once described marriage as three weeks of curiosity, three months of love, and thirty years of tolerance. Someone else described marriage as a proposition ending in a sentence. One comic said the honeymoon was the interval between the man's "I do" and the wife's "You'd better!" Still another said, "After man came woman, and she's been coming after him ever since."

I remember hearing the story of a man who was asked about the success of his long-term marriage. He responded, "The secret to our marriage is this: We never have any extended arguments. Whenever my wife gets upset, she takes out her frustrations by rearranging the furniture in the house. Whenever I get upset, I go outside and take a long walk. The secret to our marriage is this: I have substantially led an outdoor life."

> "He who knows
> he is loved
> can be content
> with
> a piece of bread,
> while all
> the luxuries of the
> world
> cannot satisfy
> the cravings of
> the lonely."
>
> FRANCES J. ROBERTS

I don't endorse these portraits of marriage, but I am sure we would not laugh at these quips if there were not at least a hint of truth in them. Sometimes we create humor to lessen the tensions we cannot control. Have you ever noticed that most of the birthday cards for people over fifty are humorous? It's as if laughing at ourselves makes aging less painful. We do the same thing with our marriages!

But let's be honest; when your marriage is falling apart, it's not a laughing matter. When you look up one day and realize you are living with someone you hardly know, it's not funny. For a marriage to be an encouragement zone, there has to be a closeness, an intimacy.

The words of Genesis 2:24 certainly speak of intimacy: "Therefore a man shall leave his father and mother and be joined to his wife, and they shall become one flesh."

When the New Testament quotes this passage, the word it uses for "joined" can also be translated, "glue." When I first saw this translation, I couldn't help but think, *That's what's missing in so many marriages today—the glue.* Nothing is holding some couples together. They do not have the resources necessary for holding the relationship together for the long run.

And here's another problem. When we use the word "intimacy" today, we almost always think of the physical side of marriage. While that is certainly a part of the program, it is by no means all that the Bible has in mind when it speaks of a couple being "glued together."

Commonly, when speaking of marriage, the term "intimacy" is used in reference to sexual intimacy exclusively. Our day has strangely majored on a minor in the matter of sexual intimacy. This is only one of the many areas of married life where intimacy can be experienced, so that consistently to restrict the meaning of the word to sexual intimacy is to expose a deficiency in the popular concept of what marriage really is. All too often the romantic illusion that intimacy is created and sustained by the sexual union obscures the higher possibility of achieving intimacy throughout the whole range of the personal relationship in marriage.[10]

Intimacy is not just body-to-body, but soul-to-soul and spirit-to-spirit.

The lack of intimacy can be traced, for many couples, back to the dating relationship where the process of bonding was totally reversed. I am convinced that God intends for couples to grow toward intimacy in a set progression. First, there needs to be spirit-to-spirit union. In one of his letters to the Corinthian Church, Paul confronted this responsibility at the most basic level:

> Do not be unequally yoked together with unbelievers. For what fellowship has righteousness with lawlessness? And what communion has light with darkness?" (2 Corinthians 6:14).

After pastoring a church for more than twenty-five years, I can give certain testimony to the struggle for intimacy in a marriage between a believer and an unbeliever. Dozens of men and women have described to me the emptiness they feel in their marriages because they have nothing in common spiritually with their spouse. It truly is difficult for two to walk together if they are not in agreement (Amos 3:3).

After spirit-to-spirit union has been established, the next level of intimacy should be soul-to-soul. This is the opportunity a couple has to get to really know each other's personality…to learn his or her disposition and character qualities…to become good friends who truly enjoy being with each other socially.

Then, finally, after the marriage, there is the body-to-body intimacy as the physical union is established.

Disastrously, the world has reversed this procedure. Too often, the process starts with a sexual encounter early in the relationship. Then perhaps a friendship begins to develop and the couple begins to live together. Sometimes, almost as an afterthought, the pair attends church and become aware of their spiritual bankruptcy. If they accept Christ into their lives, they have to go back to the beginning and start all over, this time really getting to know each other as God intended!

Recently I saw a documentary about a man who had four wives in four parts of the country. None of the wives knew about the others. The man would make up excuses about business trips and shuttle back and forth from wife to wife. Finally—and this is not hard to believe—the man had a heart attack and died. All four of his wives found out at the same time about his polygamy. As the film ended, I remember saying to my wife, "How in the world could a woman live with a man and not know he was doing this?"

But if the only "intimacy" in a marriage is "body-to-body," if there is no closeness of soul-to-soul and spirit-to-spirit, then it is truly possible to live with someone and not really know him or her at all!

A COMMITMENT TO TRANSPARENCY

In the beginning, the first married couple had no self-consciousness. They were totally selfless. No sense of embarrassment plagued them. "They were both naked, the man and his wife, and were not ashamed" (Genesis 2:25).

Then sin entered into the world (Genesis 3) and the great cover-up began. When Adam and Eve sinned, they realized they were naked, "and they sewed fig leaves together and made themselves coverings" (Genesis 3:7).

The nakedness that our first parents felt was emotional, psychological, and most of all, spiritual. Before sin and self took over, they were both naked and were not ashamed. Afterwards, everything changed.

It is not my purpose here to delve into the theology of this passage of Scripture, but I must apply its wisdom to our modern marriages. Most of us would like to reveal who we really are to the ones with whom we live, but we are afraid. We think, *If my spouse knew me as I know me, she wouldn't love me.* So we continue to provide coverings for ourselves to hide behind.

This is doubly tragic, because in most cases, we would be accepted and loved if we would just give ourselves up to one another. In his book, *Mortal Lessons: Notes in the Art of Surgery,* Dr. Richard Selzer tells about a young married couple who refused to let their transparency be destroyed even in the aftermath of disfiguring surgery:

> I stand by the bed where a young woman lies, her face post-operative, her mouth twisted in palsy, clownish. A tiny twig of the facial nerve, the one to the muscles of her mouth, has been severed. She will be thus from now on. The surgeon has followed with religious fervor the curve of her flesh; I promise you that. Nevertheless, to remove the tumor in her cheek, I had cut the little nerve.
>
> Her young husband is in the room. He stands on the opposite side of the bed, and together they seem to dwell in the evening lamplight, isolated from me, private. Who are they, I ask myself, he and this wry-mouth I have made, who gaze at and touch each other so generously, greedily? The young woman speaks.
>
> "Will my mouth always be like this?" she asks.
>
> "Yes," I say, "it will. It is because the nerve was cut."
>
> She nods, and is silent. But the young man smiles.
>
> "I like it," he says. "It is kind of cute."
>
> All at once I know who he is. I understand, and I lower my gaze. Unmindful, he bends to kiss her crooked mouth, and I so close can see how he twists his own lips to accommodate to hers, to show her that their kiss still works.[11]

This blessed couple connected at the point of potential misunderstanding and lifted each other up. Through responsibility, intimacy and transparency, they found the encouragement zone...and so can you!

LOVE IN ACTION

Standing outside of their Houston home, Jeneanne Sims kissed her husband off to work about 10:00 P.M. on September 5, 1991. As she walked back into the house she heard three gunshots, and running back outside, she collapsed to the ground beside her wounded husband. She held him until he died a few minutes later.

Some months later Jeneanne wrote:

What do I miss most? A thousand things! After thirty-one years together, I miss his warmth and gentleness and the place I had in his arms...I miss holding hands with him in worship services...I miss hearing him say, "My pretty precious one, I love you!"...I miss the pager he gave me so he could say "I love you" while I was busy at work...I miss his playfulness, his willingness to entertain a whim and go for a hamburger at three o'clock in the morning...I miss sitting for hours in the middle of the day talking, laughing, playing, sharing...I miss preparing his favorite meal...I miss his slightly off-key rendition of "Jeanie with the Light Brown Hair."

Whatever it is that we would miss if our spouse were to be taken from us, we ought not to miss in everyday love, affirmation, and encouragement. Jeneanne admonishes couples who still have each other: "Lavish him with praise and gratitude when he does something for you—even if it's nothing special! Believe me, it is special!"[12]

CHILDREN NEED CHEERLEADERS

CHILDREN NEED CHEERLEADERS

It happened around noon on Mother's Day. According to a national news report, twenty-seven-year-old Michael Murray decided to take his two children to the medical center in Massachusetts where their mother was on duty as a surgical nurse. The family wanted to drop off some Mother's Day presents: a gold necklace with the words "Number 1 Mom," and a single rose. With their mission accomplished, the father and his two children made their way back to the darkened indoor garage where the car had been parked.

Murray gently set the infant seat and three-month-old Matthew on the sun roof of the car and turned his attention to buckling Matthew's twenty-month-old sister into her seat. Without thinking further, Murray slid into the driver's seat and drove off, forgetting that Matthew was still on the roof.

Moving slowly from the darkened garage into the bright sunlight, Murray drove through busy streets toward Interstate 290. Despite heavy traffic, nobody beeped or waved to warn him that anything was wrong. Pulling onto the expressway that cuts through the city, the driver accelerated to 50 mph and then he heard it, a scraping on the roof of his car as the tiny seat with Matthew strapped in began to slide. He said, "I looked to where Matthew should have been in the car, and then in the rear view mirror I saw him sliding down the highway in his infant seat." That's where he landed. In the middle of the interstate, in the path of oncoming traffic.

THE YOUNG AND THE UNPROTECTED

Three-month-old Matthew is a picture of the generation of children growing up in our world—sliding down the highway, unprotected, heading toward oncoming traffic…and no one seems to notice. Never has there been a generation which has suffered the problems plaguing children today. Violence in American homes and in the streets is increasing alarmingly. It has reached epidemic proportions and now disrupts millions of lives.

> "We like someone
> because.
> We love someone
> although."
> HENRI DE MONTHERLANT

Children are victimized at school, at home, and in their neighborhoods. An incredible number of youngsters are beaten, maimed, molested, or even murdered by their parents. You may have seen the news story of the Chicago parents who went on vacation and left their kids home alone. After that story hit the press, many more accounts of "home-alone kids" made national news.

More than three decades have passed since U.S. divorce rates began to escalate. The statistics are in. We can now make some definitive statements about the impact divorce has had upon our culture and especially upon our children. In an article titled, "Dan Quayle Was Right," *The Atlantic Monthly* published its findings:

According to a growing body of social-scientific evidence, children in families disrupted by divorce and out-of-wedlock birth do worse than children in intact families on several measures of well-being. Children in single-parent families are six times as likely to be poor. They are also likely to stay poor longer. Twenty-two percent of children in one-parent families will experience poverty during childhood for seven years or more, as compared with only two percent of children in two-parent families.

A 1988 survey by the national Center for Health Statistics found that children in single-parent families are two to three times as likely as children in two-parent families to have emotional and behavioral problems. They are also more likely to drop out of high school, to get pregnant as teenagers, to abuse drugs, and to be in trouble with the law. Compared with children in intact families, children from disrupted families are at a much higher risk for physical or sexual abuse.... Contrary to popular belief, many children do not "bounce back" after divorce or remarriage.[1]

Children in this country are in trouble because families in this country are in trouble. And frankly, many families are in trouble because a lot of churches are in trouble. The disturbing news that I have been reading recently points out that there is little, if any, statistical difference between Christians and non-Christians regarding many areas of home life. As God's people, we must realize that good families do not "just happen." The relationship between parents and children requires the same kind of discipline and effort that is required of husbands and wives.

In this chapter I want to discuss how we parents can learn to be better encouragers of our children. If you have read what I have written so far, you will understand why I believe this to be so important. I am convinced that children who do not have cheerleading parents will have a difficult time succeeding, no matter what their family makeup. They need all the encouragement we can give them. The time has come for us to get off their back and on their team.

FOUR WAYS TO ENCOURAGE YOUR CHILDREN

There are no doubt an unlimited number of ways to encourage our children, but let's emphasize four areas that are especially crucial.

1. Focused Attention

In an article titled, "Dear Dads: Save Your Sons," written by Texas psychologist Christopher Bacorn, this issue is placed squarely at the feet of the fathers:

> What would happen if the truant fathers of America began spending time with their children? It wouldn't eliminate world hunger, but it might save some families from sinking below the poverty line. It wouldn't bring peace to the Middle East, but it just might keep a few kids from trying to find a sense of belonging with their local street-corner gang. It might not defuse the population bomb, but it just might prevent a few teenage pregnancies.
>
> If these fathers were to spend more time with their children, it just might have an effect on the future of marriage and divorce. Not only do boys lack a sense of how a man should behave; many girls don't know either, having little exposure themselves to healthy male-female relationships. With their fathers around, many young women might come to expect more than the myth that a man's chief purpose on earth is to impregnate them and then disappear. If that would happen, the next generation of absentee fathers might never come to pass.[2]

The one thing which adversely affects most families is the lack of focused attention on children. Good people, godly people—but often very busy people—allow their children to grow up without taking the time to make each child a priority. Parents live their lives and the kids come and go. Periodically there is a conversation about something which needs to be taken care of, but there seems to be no time for the kids, no time to focus attention on the children.

In his book *Creative Brooding,* Robert Rains reproduces the following letter written by a runaway son to his parents:

Dear Folks,

Thank you for everything, but I'm going to Chicago and try to start some kind of new life for myself. You ask me why I did those things that got me in trouble, why I gave you so much static while I was at home. The answer is easy for me to give you. But I don't know if you'll understand.

Remember when I was about 6 or 7 years old and I used to want you just to listen to me? I remember all the nice things you gave me for Christmas and my birthday, and I was really happy with those things for about a week...but the rest of the time during the year all I wanted was you. I just wanted you to listen to me like I was somebody who felt things. Because I remember when I was young, I felt things. But you always were busy. You never seemed to have time.

Mom, you're a wonderful cook and you always have everything so clean, and you were tired from doing all those things that made you busy. But you know something, Mom? I would have liked crackers and peanut butter just as well if you'd only sat down with me a while during the day and said to me, "Tell me all about it. Maybe I can help you understand."

I think that all the kids who are doing so many things that grown-ups are tearing out their hair worrying about are really looking for somebody who will have time to listen a few minutes, and who will really treat them as they would a grown-up who might be useful to them, you know.

Well, if anybody asks you where I am, just tell them I've gone looking for somebody with time 'cause I've got a lot of things I want to talk about.

Love to you all,

Your Son[3]

Earlier we mentioned Susanna Wesley. She gave birth to nineteen children, ten of whom grew to adulthood. Susanna "home schooled" her children during their elementary years. The boys in the family were so well prepared by their mother's instruction that they were able to go to Oxford University at the age of sixteen, with but one year of preparatory school. John Wesley became the founder of the Methodist Church. Charles, the celebrated hymn writer, composed over five thousand hymns. Samuel, another brother, was a scholarly priest of the Church of England.

> "Don't scold your children so much that they become discouraged and quit trying."
> COLOSSIANS 3:21, TLB

And one daughter, Martha, was a member of the inner circle of the famous lexicographer, Dr. Samuel Johnson.

In a letter written by Susanna to her son John, she told of her relationship with the children. "I take as much time as I can spare every night to talk with each child apart. On Monday I talk with Molly; on Tuesday with Hetty; Wednesday with Nancy; Thursday with Jacky; Friday with Patty; Saturday with Charles; and Emily and Suky together on Sunday." Each child had his or her day. Once, when her famous son John struggled with a difficult situation, he wrote to his mother, "Oh, Mother, what I'd give for a Thursday evening!"[4]

Most of us do not have unlimited time to give to our kids. But we shouldn't allow the Enemy to persuade us that if we don't have a lot of time, we can't give *any* time. We must take the time we have and use it the very best way we can in order to make an impact on the precious ones God has put under our care. I am so impressed with our Lord in this regard.

Jesus faced an incredible schedule. There were meetings, confrontations, and training sessions with the disciples. There were long walks, big decisions, magnificent healings. The disciples were overwhelmed by what Jesus accomplished. But He always had time for individuals. He always gave them His full attention. Even when dying on the cross for the whole world, our Lord took the time to help one individual find his way to the Kingdom of God.

One of the most encouraging things a parent can do is to take a chapter from Susanna Wesley's book and give each child a day or an hour that belongs just to him or her. Many parents tell me that bedtime provides the best opportunity to converse, encourage, and pray with each of their children.

2. Individual Affirmation

Each child needs to understand his uniqueness. He needs to know he is special and unlike any other child God ever created. Solomon reminds us in one of his well-known proverbs that we must study the uniqueness of each child so we will be able to properly train him. "Train up a child in the way he should go and when he is old he will not depart from it" (Proverbs 22:6).

Several years ago I wrote a book on the family titled *Exposing the Myths of Parenthood*. In that book I dealt with this verse from the Old Testament:

> The Hebrew word or phrase for "in the way" describes the habit or character of an individual at his own age level. The emphasis is on the importance of adjusting our training according to the ability of a child at each stage in his

development. Children do not come in standard packages; each child is different, and we parents need to study the "labels." Bringing up a child in the way he should go is not an unchangeable mathematical equation. Comparing one child with another is like buying two products in the market: they may be processed by the same manufacturer, have similar boxes, but taste entirely different. Each child has his own way, and by listening, or even keeping a diary of behavior patterns, we can begin to determine what that way is.... Parenting is not an easy formula. The Bible gives us the major principles, but the application is different for everyone.[5]

No doubt you have heard horror stories of parents who ask their kids, "Why aren't you like your brother?" The child usually says, "I'm not like him because I'm not him!" Every child is created uniquely by God. God puts a certain formula in the heart of every child and it is the parents' challenge to figure out the combination. We need to spend time studying, looking, listening, and observing.

One father I know keeps a notebook on his kids. He writes down the insights he gets into his children's lives which will help him figure out the combinations to their hearts. He does this so he will know how to best serve them and lead them in the way they should go.

Ruth Stafford Peale gives this advice for encouraging the uniqueness in our children:

The secret is this: watch to see where a child's innate skills or talents lie, then gently (do not expect too much too soon) lead or coax him or her in those areas. It may be difficult for a father who was a crack athlete to understand and help a son who would rather play chess than football. But chess, not football, is what such a boy needs if confidence is to grow in him. If he does that one thing well he will come to believe that he can do other things well, and he won't be afraid to attempt them.[6]

Children are encouraged when we affirm their originality. Some kids are athletic; some aren't. Some are musicals; some aren't. Some are introverts; others are extroverts. They are all different, but they are all gifts to us from God. As the psalmist says, they are "a heritage of the Lord" (Psalm 127:3).

One of the good friends I have made as the result of our radio program "Turning Point" is a man by the name of Tom Bisset. He is the manager of radio station WRBS-FM in Baltimore, Maryland. Recently Tom wrote a book and asked me to write a blurb for the inside cover. After reading the manuscript, I was both happy to write the recommendation and intrigued by the subject matter he so ably presented. The book is titled *Why Christian Kids Leave the Faith* and it powerfully reminds us of the importance of knowing our children and identifying their personalities.

Quoting psychiatrist Ross Campbell as his resource, Tom made this analysis of the personalities of children:

All children can be placed in one of two basic personality types: pro-authority and anti-authority. In Dr. Campbell's view, three-fourths of all children are anti-authority in their personal make-up. These are the kids who come into the world wanting to move your rules aside. The other one-fourth are pro-authority. Their basic approach to life is, "What can I do to help you, Mom and Dad?"

The central issue for parents is their understanding of each child's personality. There is no way an anti-authority child can be handled in the same way as a pro-authority child. Once again, Tom Bisset cites the tragic results of failing to understand our children:

When confronted by an anti-authoritarian child, parents often react by becoming more rigid, severe disciplinarians. They insist on their children doing exactly as they say—my way or the highway. Parents then seek to reinforce their position by taking their children to a church where the same rules apply.

Far from solving the problem of a rebellious, anti-authority child, this overly authoritarian approach creates an angry reaction which results in intense clashes in the home. And it can lead to faith rejection as well. In Dr. Campbell's opinion, the intensely authoritarian and rigidly disciplinarian approach, both at home and in church, is the principle reason so many anti-authoritarian kids "turn against the church."[7]

The root meaning for the term "train up" in Proverbs 22:6 is "palate or roof of the mouth." In Job 34:3 and Psalm 119:103, we find references to taste or "honey to the mouth." The picture is this: The Arab midwife would take olive oil or crushed dates on her finger and rub the palate of a newborn baby to create in the infant a desire to suck. The real meaning of "training" is to create a taste or desire.

Therefore, the writer of Proverbs is reminding parents that their task is to develop in their children a hunger, taste, or desire for spiritual things; to cultivate the personal urge to love God and follow Him.

I talk to Baby Boomers almost every week who are just now returning to the church. Many of them have been on long and painful journeys away from God and away from the church. They all say almost the same thing: "I went to church and I had this stuff jammed down my throat and I just had enough of it and I walked away." We need to understand our kids and learn how we can best minister to their needs. This doesn't mean always giving them what they want or letting them do anything they please. It means loving them and affirming their uniqueness. It means individual affirmation.

Brennan Bagwell and Scott Elkins wrote a song that helps us understand what's at stake here:

> She's always been a good girl,
> tried to please her mom and dad.
> She practices her music
> and does the best she can.
>
> The preacher lays the law down,
> better listen to the man,
> Just worry about obeyin'
> you don't have to understand.
>
> We've gotta give a reason,
> in a way they understand,
> Not opinion legislation that
> drives our good kids bad.
>
> The pressures and the changes
> seem to multiply with time.
> But the rules that she's obeyin'
> were never realigned.
>
> Oh, but where's the love they're needing?
> Where is the love they're seeking?
> They need our arms around them,
> not the chains that only weaken.
>
> She's standing on the edge now,
> her pretty face so sad.
> We really shouldn't wonder
> why our good kids turn out bad.

She's standing on the edge now
looking at the world.
Be careful how you push her.
You may lose your little girl.[8]

No parents set out to lose their little girl. No mom and dad try to drive away their little boy. Yet if we don't give our kids the individual affirmation they need, it happens a lot easier than you might think. So let's not let it happen.

3. Genuine Appreciation

Steve Farrar tells a wonderful story about a Texas family who took appreciation a bit too far:

A lot of rich Texans went broke in the 1980s. But there are still a few rich Texans left. One of them was recently talking to a banker in New York. After several minutes of conversation, the Texan took a liking to the New Yorker. "I've got a great idea," he said. "Why don't I send my jet up to New York this weekend to pick up you and your wife? We'd like to have you join us at our son's ranch outside of Austin. He's got 100,000 acres of land stocked with quarter horses, purebred cattle, and exotic game. Yep, I'm real proud of the boy. He earned it all by himself."

"It sounds like your son has been very successful for a young man," replied the banker. "Just out of curiosity, how old is your son?"

"He's eight," replied the Texan.

"Eight!" said the shocked banker. "How on earth did an eight-year-old boy earn enough money to buy a ranch like that?"

"He got four As and one B," replied the Texan.[9]

Most of us are not going to appreciate our children like this Texan did, but we must find our own way to communicate our love in a positive language they can understand.

Do you appreciate your kids? Colossians 3:21 says: "Fathers, do not provoke your children, lest they become discouraged." What do you think Paul meant? Another translation says, "Don't embitter your children." The text seems to be speaking of a father who governs his family by objection, a father who never notices anything except what's wrong. One of the modern translations says, "Fathers, don't hassle your kids."

Words are powerful, capable of destroying children. Used wrongly, words can become weapons and tools for getting even—and can bring a child down in a way that nothing else can.

It's a terrible thing to be in a family where the only thing parents ever notice are the things their children do wrong. Do you ever stop to think about why some kids end up doing a lot of bad things? Maybe it's the only way they ever get any attention. The only time anybody notices them is when they do something they shouldn't do.

I know of a father whose son was a good basketball player, averaging thirty points a game. But every night when the son came home, his father would say to him as he walked in the door, "How did you miss that open lay-up you had?" The only thing the father saw was the shot his son missed. He never mentioned any of the things his son did well. That's how you get a bitter-hearted child. That's how a child gets discouraged.

Spencer Johnson wrote a book called *The One Minute Manager* and followed it up with a book called *The One Minute Father*. It's a great little book. It's not a Christian book, but it mentions a Christian principle: Instead of walking around the house trying to catch your children doing bad things, walk around trying to catch them doing good things. And when they do something good, tell them you appreciate it and you are glad for it. Tell them often. Praise them often. Encourage them often.

Rich DeVoss was asked one time in a television interview, "What is the most important management skill you learned in the process of building the Amway Company?" Do you know what he said? "The most important management skill I learned was how to be a cheerleader."

There has never been a generation of young men and women who have needed parental support and encouragement like our kids today. Cheerleading parents can make lifetime contributions in the lives of their children. Our children need to know that no matter what happens in their lives, we are for them, and we will go to the wall for them. Our children need to believe: *Dad's on my team. Mom's on my team.* You can start today to be a Mom or Dad who truly communicates your love and appreciation to each child. But let me warn you ahead of time not to expect them to understand what you're doing.

I came across a story some time ago about a mother who had just finished reading a book on parenting. She was convicted about some of the things she had been failing to do as a parent. Feeling this conviction, she went upstairs to talk to her son. When she got upstairs, all she could hear coming from her boy's room was the loud sound of his drums. She had a message she wanted to deliver, but when she knocked on the door, she got cold feet.

"Got a minute?" she said, as her son answered her knock.

"Mom, you know I always have a minute for you," said the boy.

"You know, son, I...I...I just love the way you play the drums." He said, "You do? Well, thanks Mom!"

She got up and started back downstairs. Halfway down, she realized that she had not conveyed the message she had intended so back she went to his door and once again knocked. "It's Mom again! Do you have another minute?" she said.

He said, "Mom, like I told you before, I always have a minute for you."

She walked over and sat on the bed. "When I was here before I had something I wanted to tell you and I didn't get it said. What I really meant to say was...your dad and I...we just really think you're great."

He said, "You and Dad?"

She said, "Yes, your Dad and I."

"Okay, Mom. Thanks a lot."

She left and was once again halfway down the stairs when she realized she had gotten closer to the message she intended to give, but still had not told her boy that she loved him. So up the stairs once more she went and back to the door again. This time he heard her coming. Before she could ask he shouted, "Yeah, I have a minute!"

Mom sat down on the bed once more. "You know, Son, I've tried this twice now and haven't gotten it out. What I really came up here to tell you is this. I love you. I love you with all of my heart. Not Dad and I love you, but I love you."

He said, "Mom, that's great. I love you, too!" He gave her a great big hug.

She started out of the room and was back at the head of the stairs when her son stuck his head out of his room and said, "Mom, do you have a minute?"

She laughed and said, "Sure."

"Mom," he said, "did you just come back from a seminar?"

4. Physical Affection

We need to love our children in a tangible way—by what we do, by what we say, by putting our arms around them and hugging them, by letting them know they really are loved.

Many of the parents of my generation tell me they grew up in a family that did not hug or give physical affection. I don't want to indict that generation, but I do hope I have convinced you that our children's challenges are so great that we cannot run the risk of being cold and aloof! It is no longer enough to love them in our *hearts*. We must communicate that love in every possible way, including physically. In an earlier chapter I wrote about the encouragement that is wrapped up in a touch and the power that is communicated in a hug. Those concepts have special application to the parent-child relationship.

One area of physical affection is often overlooked in books on parenting, however. I think we may have long underestimated the love that is communicated when we laugh with our children. I mean truly, hilariously, boisterously laugh. My children remember most vividly the crazy things we have done together. When we review life, these are the first things we talk about. I wish there had been more of them.

Bruce Larson tells a story that will nail this thought down for all of us:

> I have a great friend down in Montgomery, Alabama, and a few years ago he told me an unforgettable story of a summer vacation he had planned for his wife and children. He was unable to go himself because of business, but he helped them plan every day of a camping trip in the family station wagon from Montgomery all the way to California, up and down the West Coast, and then back to Montgomery.
>
> He knew their route exactly and the precise time they would be crossing the Great Divide. So, my friend arranged to fly himself out to the nearest airport and hire a car and a driver to take him to a place which every car must pass. He sat by the side of the road several hours waiting for the sight of that familiar station wagon. When it came into view, he stepped out on the road and put his thumb out to hitch-

hike a ride with the family who assumed that he was 3,000 miles away.

I said to him, "Coleman, I'm surprised they didn't drive off the road in terror or drop dead of a heart attack. What an incredible story. Why did you go to all that trouble?"

"Well, Bruce," he said, "Someday I'm going to be dead, and when that happens, I want my kids and my wife to say, 'You know, Dad was a lot of fun.'"

Wow, I thought. Here's a man whose whole game plan is to make fun and happiness for other people.

It made me wonder what my family will remember about me. I'm sure they will say, "Well, Dad was a nice guy, but he sure worried a lot about putting out the lights and closing the windows and picking up around the house and cutting the grass." But I'd also like them to be able to say that Dad was the guy who made life a lot of fun.[10]

I imagine when Coleman's children talk about life with father, that story is one of the first to be told. When we enjoy life with our children, we say to them that they are special to us…that we love them and enjoy being with them. It is a message that always gets through!

All of us who are still in the parenting process need to look beyond the homes of our own childhood where physical affection was seldom expressed. Maybe we shook hands with our fathers and kissed our mothers on the cheek. But we're in a different generation, and if ever there was a time when physical affection was a parental priority, this is that time!

ENCOURAGING YOUR CHILDREN

Although there are a myriad ways to love and encourage our children, four of the most critical occur when we give them

* *focused attention*—giving them our time and making them a priority;

* *individual affirmation*—accepting and encouraging their unique personalities and traits;

* *genuine appreciation*—looking for the good instead of the bad and being on their team;

* *physical affection*—letting them know, in ways they can feel, that they're important.

To be sure, there are many other things we can and should do to help our children become all God meant them to be. But these four areas provide a great place to start. We can't go too far wrong if we commit ourselves to following through in each of these critical arenas.

THE REST OF THE STORY

I can't close this chapter without telling you what happened to little Matthew Murray, the baby whose harried dad drove off with Matthew perched in his car seat atop of the vehicle. You'll recall that the car seat flew off the roof, hit the road and was sliding down the highway almost as fast as the cars were coming toward it. An antique dealer named James Boothby was following the Murray car when he saw the whole event unfold. He saw young Matthew sail off the roof and hit the road. He recalled:

> I saw something in the air. At first I thought someone had thrown some garbage out the window. Then I saw it and thought it was a doll. Then the doll opened its mouth, and I realized this was a little baby. It just landed on the road. It bounced a couple of times, and it never tipped over. It just landed on the road and slid along a bit. I slammed on my car brakes and turned my car around in the lane so that no other cars could go by. I jumped from the car, and I ran and found an uninjured baby in an undamaged car seat, and

scooped him up in my arms and took him back and gave him to his petrified father.

That true story has to be as close to a grade A miracle as anything you and I have ever experienced. God intervened in that situation to prevent a horrible tragedy.

Just as God obviously intervened in that potential disaster, I am convinced that God wants to intervene in our families. But He's probably not going to do something so spectacular. What He is going to do, before He changes our families, is change *us*. He will make us the kind of person we ought to be. And by His grace, we can be the kind of parent we want to be.

LOVE IN ACTION

Second only to drug concerns, parents are most frustrated about their inability to talk to their children. Out of a thousand girls surveyed by a teen publication, less than one-third said they confided in their mothers.

Children do things that leave us shaking our heads. Such occasions are frightening and baffling. We want to reach out to help, but don't know how. Will we make the problem worse with our awkward attempts to talk? We grope for answers, not always sure of the questions. So what's a parent to do?

Being a successful parent requires that you speak two languages—*yours* and *theirs.* Being your best means knowing when to pay attention to your child as well as reading the real meaning behind his words—or lack of them. Since kids don't always say exactly what they mean, fluency in the language of "parent-ese" helps decipher their true feelings.

Parent-ese is not a dialect you can master in a year or so. Unlike conventional languages, the vocabulary changes. It's an expression of more *emotions,* fewer *words.* Mastery of nouns and verbs is less important than deciphering the emotions masked behind the nouns and verbs.

Make an effort to develop an attitude, a tone of voice, empathy, and sincerity that says, *I love you no matter what happens.* Be courageous enough to confide your disappointments, hopes, and feelings in your child. They never grow too old to be told they are loved. Make it a way of life—not just an occasional verbal pat on the head.

Parent-ese translates parental love into action.[11]

THE WRITE WAY TO ENCOURAGE

THE WRITE WAY TO ENCOURAGE

The Bowery district of Chicago is home to a famous landmark: The Pacific Garden Mission. If you listen to Christian radio, you may have heard a program originated at the Pacific Garden Mission called "Unshackled." This program tells stories of men and women whose lives have been changed through this ministry, a ministry in the most rundown part of Chicago.

As unlikely as it might seem, the Pacific Garden Mission takes its name from its previous tenant, the Pacific Beer Garden. The mission provides hope, shelter, food, and clothing for the street people of Chicago. It's a place where hope is offered to those who are often hopeless. Sarah Clark and her husband, who founded the ministry, began by printing little cards on which appeared this message: "Hope for all who enter. Pacific Garden Mission—67 West Van Buren Street. Strangers and poor always welcome. Special song service, 7:30 every night." They took these little invitation cards out in the districts around the mission and distributed them to all the street people they could find.

That little card made a big difference in many lives. Some folks who got the card visited the mission that same night. Some of them, while they were there, were introduced to the hope found in Christ.

Many of those who didn't show up the first night took the invitation cards, crumpled them up, and stuck them down in their pockets, only to find them later when they were in need. In desperation they made their ways to the Pacific Garden Mission...and received help.

A TRANSFUSION OF COURAGE

Each of us lives some of our days in the war zone. Weekly we face battles, challenges, and shock. When we see the missiles whizzing by overhead, we need someone who will encourage us. Encouragement is transfusing some of your courage into another life. The Bible says, "In the last days perilous times will come" (2 Timothy 3:1). The Book of Hebrews says we ought to be more and more involved in encouragement as those days approach. When the perilous times increase and the battles intensify, we will need encouragement more than ever.

> "I've got it all synthesized into one major statement. Here is what you need to do if you have adolescents: 'Just get them through it.'"
>
> JAMES DOBSON

One of the motivations behind Paul's letters to the New Testament churches was his desire to encourage his friends. These early believers were members of churches scattered throughout the ancient Roman Empire, a time ruled by cruelty and persecution. These persecuted, isolated followers of Christ, trying to make their way in the world, often met in caves and the catacombs of Rome for mutual encouragement. They faced life-threatening challenges every day. Paul, who founded most of these churches, wrote to communicate his heart to them. In the beginning verses of almost every one of his letters, Paul labors to deliver a word of hope and affirmation.

Let me say first of all that wherever I go I hear you being talked about! For your faith in God is becoming known around the world. How I thank God through Jesus Christ for this good report, and for each one of you. God knows how often I pray for you. Day and night I bring you and your needs in prayer to the one I serve with all of my might (Romans 1:8–9, TLB).

If you received a letter like that from Paul, wouldn't you be encouraged? To know that he put you on his prayer list and prayed for you every day and every night?

I can never stop thanking God for all the wonderful gifts he has given you, now that you are Christ's; he has enriched your whole life. He has helped you to speak out for him and has given you a full understanding of the truth; what I told you Christ could do for you has happened! Now you have every grace and blessing; every spiritual gift and power for doing his will.... He guarantees right up to the end that you will be counted free from all sin and guilt on that day when he returns. God will surely do this for you, for he always does just what he says, and he is the one who invited you into this wonderful friendship with his Son, even Christ our Lord (1 Corinthians 1:4–9, TLB).

Wow! What power there is in a word of encouragement.

What a wonderful God we have—he is the Father of our Lord Jesus Christ, the source of every mercy, and the one who so wonderfully comforts and strengthens us in our hardships and trials. And why does he do this? So that when others are troubled, needing our sympathy and encouragement, we can pass on to them the same help and comfort God has given us. You can be sure that the more we undergo sufferings for Christ, the more he will shower us with his comfort and encouragement (2 Corinthians 1:3–5, TLB).

WRITTEN ENCOURAGEMENT

Much of the early church's encouragement was passed from one person to another through writing. When they were together in their assemblies, they verbally encouraged one another. But between those risky and infrequent meetings, they depended heavily on written words of hope.

Written encouragement is one of the most effective tools God has given to His children. Since you are reading this book, I know you have the ability to write encouragement upon the hearts of others. Consider now at least five ways that written encouragement can be a powerful influence for good in the lives of those you love.

1. Written encouragement is deliberate

Written encouragement conveys a careful, prayerful, thoughtful investment of time. When you receive a written note, you know someone had to sit down and organize his thoughts to convey his love and encouragement to you. That means something!

How different that is from the "syrupy" encouragement we sometimes receive. There are some "warm, fuzzy" people whom I call strokers. I've been around some who stroke you so much that, if for one minute they stop stroking, you wonder what's wrong. Frankly, after awhile, their words often lose their purpose and meaning.

Written encouragement seldom falls into that trap. It's like the old saying, "It's not the gift, it's the journey." I've always understood that to mean something like this: Beyond the value of the gift is the perceived effort its giving required.

Last year I drove to one of my favorite mountain hide-aways…a beautiful California village called Julian. I made that journey with one purpose: To buy some pies. I went to the Julian Pie Factory and bought twenty pies! Then I brought them home and gave (most of) them to special friends. It was fun to give away a pie in a box which said "Julian Pie Factory." You see, the pie was only half the gift—the other half was the journey to get it.

That's the way it is with written encouragement. Often more important than what you say is the deliberate effort you made to make the statement. It means a great deal that you took the time to express your thoughts in writing.

2. Written encouragement is definite

Have you ever meant to write a note, but you failed to go through with it? Or meant to say a word of encouragement, but just didn't bump into the person that week? Or meant to call someone, but never got around to it? That happens in all of our lives. What we're going to do sometime, we end up doing no time.

But a word of written encouragement is a definite moment. You can write a note of encouragement any time, whether the person is with you or not. And when it is done, it is done!

3. Written encouragement is direct

Verbal encouragement is not always direct. Often our spoken words are covered up by our personal inhibitions. Do you always say to others the positive things you want to say? If you do, you're very unusual. Often we say only what we think we can get by with, or what we feel comfortable saying. This even happens in our families.

Paul was a great hero of the New Testament. Outside of Jesus Christ, he probably had the greatest impact on the church of any single individual. But Paul also had a reputation as a meek man. In one of his letters, he wrote, "I am meek when I am face to face with you, but bold towards you when I am absent" (2 Corinthians 10:1). People accused Paul of being timid when face-to-face with them.

Are you like that? You have your words all planned out...until you stand face-to-face, when suddenly all your words turn to mush.

Writing removes that obstacle. You can write without intimidation. Alone in a special, quiet place, you can say what's really in your heart. I have said important things to my father in writing that I've never been able to express verbally. Written encouragement comes directly from the heart, uninterrupted and unhindered. That's why it's so powerful.

4. Written encouragement is durable

Written encouragement keeps on encouraging long after the note/letter/poem is written and sent. I still have the first encouragement note I ever received. It's yellow by now. The date on the letter is February 26, 1941; I was born on the thirteenth of February that same year. I was only thirteen days old when this letter was written. The author of that note was Earl G. Griffith, one of my father's closest friends. Here's what he wrote:

> Master David Paul Jeremiah:
> My Dear David, it is quite beyond me to tell you how glad I am to welcome you to our country, to my native state, to dear old Toledo, Ohio, and to the Emmanuel Baptist Church, to the parsonage where we spent so many delightful years, and to the alumni of the Baptist Bible Seminary. I trust all of these allegiances will not confuse you, being so young. Here is hoping that you will live up to your name, as I am confident you will. You certainly made the best possible choice as to parentage. And you can well follow in the footsteps of your mother on everything, even as to appearance, and of your father on everything, except the matter of attention given to your hair. It is better to comb it occasionally.
> Here's hoping that your dad is as well as can be expected.

My best to your lassie sister, to your neighbors, to all our good friends at Emmanuel. Come and see us and bring the other three members of the family. Also bring a bottle of Verner's Ginger Ale. Lenten will soon be over. Happy days and many of them. The Lord bless you.

P.S. The card your father sent us said you weighed about 960 pounds. That seems a little heavy, but perhaps it was ministerially speaking.

I've pulled this letter out several times throughout my life to be reminded of Earl, his love for my family, and his early encouragement in my life. Written encouragement never dies! If you speak a word of encouragement, it may not last long. But when you write a note, it lives forever.

Do you keep special notes written to you over the years? Do you ever pull them out and read them? I once received a note I will never throw away. It came from a man in my church and was written to me when a friend of mine (another pastor) had failed morally and had lost his church. In this note, the man told me how much he loved me. He told me he and his wife had prayed for us as a family regularly. He mentioned each of our family members by name. And then he challenged me to maintain a life of purity and godliness. Last, he signed his name.

> *"When they read the letter they rejoiced over its encouragement."*
> Acts 15:31

I will never throw that note away!

Do you keep love letters from your spouse? Perhaps you've heard the story about the little boy who came home one day and said, "Mommy, I've had a great day!"

"You have?" she asked.

"Yep."

"And what have you been doing?"

"I've been playing postman."

"You have?"

"Yep. I put a letter in every mail box on this block."

"Well, Honey, where did you get the letters?"

"I found them in your top dresser drawer, wrapped up in a pink ribbon."

We all keep things which are important to us. (And my guess is that, after reading this story, some of you with little children at home will check the security of your dresser drawer!)

5. Written encouragement is distance-proof

Our church missionaries tell me that one of the most important days on the mission field is mail-call day. They look forward to that day and often go to the landing strip to wait for hours until the plane comes in. They tell me that one encouraging letter from home often provides encouragement for them and dozens of their co-workers. Although I live in San Diego, California, I can write a note to someone in Togo, Africa, and all the distance between us vanishes into nothingness when the envelope is opened and words of encouragement are read. Written encouragement is distance-proof.

My eldest daughter, Jan, lived in the Dominican Republic during a very important time in her life. I am grateful that while she was there, she wrote to us every week. I have never read letters like I read those letters. I read in between each line for any little indication of how she was doing. I read them often, and they encouraged my heart.

A MODERN-DAY EXAMPLE

In the book *Loving God,* author Charles Colson tells the story of an incredible ninety-one-year-old woman, known affectionately as Grandma Howell.[1] If anyone ever lived out the power of written encouragement, it was Myrtle Howell.

As she moved into the twilight of her life, she had more than one reason to let depression take over, to give up and die. Her youngest son was deceased. Her oldest son was in declining health. Many of her friends were dying and she had begun to believe she had nothing left to live for. One day she prayed with all of her heart and told the Lord that if He didn't have anything more for her to do, she was ready to die.

According to Grandma Howell, God spoke to her in three words: "Write to prisoners." After arguing with the Lord about her lack of education and her age, Myrtle wrote her first letter:

> Dear Inmate,
>
> I am a grandmother who loves and cares for you who is in a place you had not plans to be.
>
> My love and sympathy goes out to you. I am willing to be a friend to you in correspondence. If you'd like to hear from me, write me. I will answer every letter you write.
>
> A Christian Friend,
> Grandmother Howell[2]

Upon receiving her letter, the prison chaplain at the Atlanta Penitentiary sent Myrtle the names of eight prison inmates. That was the beginning of an unbelievable ministry of encouragement. Over the next months, this elderly woman carried on an extensive written ministry with hundreds of incarcerated men and women— and all of it was done from her little room in a high-rise home for the aged in Columbus, Georgia.

According to Colson, writing to the prisoners was only half of Myrtle's joy. They wrote back! And their letters were warm, rich epistles of gratitude. One inmate who signed her name "Grandmother Janice" wrote:

> Dear Grandmother,
>
> I received your letter and it made me sad when you

wrote that you think you may not be alive much longer. I thought that I would wait and come to see you and then tell you all you have meant to me. But now I've changed my mind. I'm going to tell you now.

You've given me all the love and concern and care that I've missed for years and my whole outlook on life has changed. You've made me realize that life is worth living and that it's not all bad. You claim it's all God's doing, but I think you deserve the credit.

I didn't think I was capable of feeling love for anyone again, but I know I love you as my very own precious grandmother.[3]

This story has made a deep impression on my heart. No one is ever too old to encourage others. Just think what would happen to the many hurting people of this world if Grandma Howell's example was emulated. And just imagine what would happen to the "Grandma Howells" of the world! According to Myrtle, "Writing to inmates has filled my last days with joy....These last years have been the most fulfilling of my whole life."[4]

There is incredible power in written encouragement. Do you know somebody who needs a word of encouragement? We all have friends who are going through difficult times. Why not take the time right now to think of somebody you know who needs a word of encouragement? And while you are motivated and thinking about it, write a note to that person. There is great joy in the ministry of written encouragement...on both sides of the pen.

LOVE IN ACTION

Written applause carries a special power all its own. It confirms that honesty and goodwill have exerted tangible, visible effort. It can be relished repeatedly, making the acknowledgment seem permanent and official.

Penned praise is often easier to accept. We can savor the flavor without distraction. It is not necessary to invent some socially acceptable response. The moment belongs solely to the reader. And it is delicious!

The price of a first-class stamp has changed—but human relations have not. People still require recognition and appreciation. If we can provide that, new motivation is born within the hearts of the discouraged and unappreciated. With renewed courage, they are empowered to try again and finally achieve.

Even with the price of postage escalating annually, mailbox philanthropy is still the bargain of the century. Bestow a priceless gift that is worth everything. For mere pennies, dispense your own bit of good will in an envelope. Be a pocket-change philanthropist. We often claim there just isn't time for completing all our best intentions. "Happy is the person who discovers there isn't time left for not doing them!"

Five minutes, a first-class stamp, and your personal expression can spark a brighter, richer life. Bestow your fortune on others. Cultivate a conscious awareness of the good around you. In spite of the bumper stickers that would have us believe otherwise, good happens! Lots of it. Look for it in the actions of others. Take out your ever-ready pen and document it.

Start now in the "write" direction![5]

WITH FRIENDS LIKE THESE...

WITH FRIENDS LIKE THESE...

One day Satan was in the presence of God and God said to him, "Have you considered my servant Job, that there is none like him on the earth, a blameless and upright man, one who fears God and shuns evil?" (Job 1:8).

In essence, Satan replied, "Well, God, that is understandable. I mean, You put a hedge around Job. You've given him all the good things he has. Anybody would be good and upright and shun evil if they had everything Job has." So God said, "I'll tell you what, Satan. I'll let you destroy everything he has, but you can't take his life."

So God allowed Job's suffering—not to tempt Job to do wrong, but to demonstrate Job's integrity. God allowed Job's hardship to prove to Satan and to us that we can take the worst hits life can throw at us and still keep our integrity. So Satan left God's presence, determined to bring Job down.

AN UPRIGHT MAN DOWN IN THE DUMPS

In one day, Job lost everything. One after another, four frightened messengers reported to Job that five hundred yoke of oxen, five hundred donkeys, and three thousand camels were stolen by enemies in a raid. Seven thousand sheep were struck by lightening and killed. And all ten of Job's children—seven sons and three daughters—were killed when a tornado hit the house in which they were staying. All but four of Job's servants were also killed. And all heaven watched to see what Job would do.

Then Job arose, tore his robe, and shaved his head; and he fell to the ground and worshiped. And he said: "Naked I came from my mother's womb, and naked shall I return there. The LORD gave, and the LORD has taken away; blessed be the name of the LORD." And in all this Job did not sin nor charge God with wrong (Job 1:20–22).

> "Love is like the five loaves and two fishes. It doesn't start to multiply until you give it away."

Chalk one up for God and one strike against Satan. Satan came back and said (my paraphrase), "God, let me tell You. I understand that Job didn't cave in when he lost everything. But if you touch his life, if you make him sick, he will surely curse you." So God said, "All right, Satan, round two. You can do anything you want to him, but you can't kill him."

Have you ever been so sick you thought you were going to die—and then you were afraid you wouldn't? That's what happened to Job. We don't know what sicknesses hit him, but we do know the symptoms: Severe itching, insomnia, running sores and scabs, nightmares, bad breath, weight loss, chills and fever, diarrhea, and blackened skin that literally fell off his body. Job was so mutilated by his illness that when his three closest friends saw him, they didn't recognize him.

And Job's wife? She hadn't been in the house when it caved in on the children. She was still alive, but she wasn't much help to Job. When Job got sick, she said, "Do you still hold fast to your integrity? Curse God and die!" (2:9). But he said to her, "You speak as one of the foolish women speaks. Shall we indeed accept good from God, and shall we not accept adversity?" And then the text adds, "In all this Job did not sin with his lips" (2:10).

To be fair, we don't know the motives of Job's wife. She had lost all of her children and the man she so revered, the one who had given her everything she'd ever desired, was sitting in the dump with a pottery shard in his hand, scratching his body to relieve the itching of his terrible disease. As his wife saw him out there, quite possibly she thought, *I'd rather see you dead than like you are.*

THE THREE UNWISE MEN

The kind of tragedy Job suffered would not be easy to keep quiet. So when three of his friends heard about his trouble, they agreed to meet together and visit Job.

> Now when Job's three friends heard of all this adversity that had come upon him, each one came from his own place— Eliphaz the Temanite, Bildad the Shuhite, and Zophar the Naamathite. For they had made an appointment together to come and mourn with him, and to comfort him [encourage him]. And when they raised their eyes from afar, and did not recognize him, they lifted their voices and wept; and each one tore his robe and sprinkled dust on his head toward heaven. So they sat down with him on the ground seven days and seven nights, and no one spoke a word to him, for they saw that his grief was very great (Job 2:11–13).

What did these friends do correctly? They came to Job when he was in trouble. It's easy to be a friend from far off. You hear somebody is in trouble and you commiserate with them, you feel badly for them. But these three friends got together and went to Job. That demonstrated some commitment on their part. They also had hearts of compassion. When they saw Job, they wept with him. There's probably no better salve you can pour on a hurting person's wounds than genuine tears. These friends sat down with Job and wept. And then (the wisest thing they did) they kept quiet for seven days. For seven days and seven nights they sat without saying a word. A lot of commentators have noted that they made up for it later. They sure did!

Eliphaz, Bildad, and Zophar came allegedly to comfort Job, to encourage him. But they were lousy encouragers. Actually, Job used the word "miserable" (that's Old Testament for lousy).

> Then Job answered and said: "I have heard many such things; miserable comforters are you all! Shall words of wind have an end? Or what provokes you that you answer? I also could speak as you do, if your soul were in my soul's place. I could heap up words against you, and shake my head at you; but I would strengthen you with my mouth, and the comfort of my lips would relieve your grief" (Job 16:1–5).

Job said, in effect, "Listen, just suppose our roles were reversed. Suppose I were to say all the things you have said, heap all these words up against you. But I don't think I'd do that. I think I'd try to really encourage you. You're all just lousy encouragers."

Have you met Eliphaz, Bildad, or Zophar? Let's meet them one at a time.

ELIPHAZ'S ERROR

Eliphaz, the first speaker, was the oldest. He based all his speeches on personal observation. Over and over he said, "I have seen...I have seen...I have seen...." Get the picture? "Job, let me tell you what I have learned about life." One of the key elements in Eliphaz' "counsel" was a terrible dream he had (4:12–21). In his dream, Eliphaz saw a spirit and was frightened by it. When Eliphaz came to comfort Job, he used his own traumatic experience in his counsel. He brought in that incident and laid it as a template over Job's problem, as if to say, "Let me tell you what I have learned through my experience, and let me show you how it relates to your suffering."

After delivering a preliminary statement, Eliphaz gives his analysis of Job's predicament.

"Remember now, who ever perished being innocent? Or where were the upright ever cut off? Even as I have seen, those who plow iniquity and sow trouble reap the same" (Job 4:7–8).

Now, don't you feel encouraged for Job? Eliphaz said, "Job, let me tell you something. Nobody who is upright ever goes through trouble like this. Job, God never punishes the righteous. Whatever a man sows by way of iniquity he always reaps. So, Job, here's the real issue: What exactly have you done which has caused this suffering in your life?"

One of the most painful things that can be afflicted on troubled people is the false guilt often heaped on them by well-meaning Christians. I come from a strong fundamentalist background and we're experts at this. We are very good at heaping guilt on people, even when we don't know the whole story.

In Job's case, we do know the story. We know his suffering didn't come because he was bad. He was suffering because he was good! In fact, he was the "goodest" person in the whole world. Eliphaz was totally mistaken.

BILDAD'S BLUNDER

Job's three friends had gotten together before they went to see Job (2:11). They probably discussed why all this calamity might have befallen their friend. So naturally there is some similarity in their analyses.

Bildad was a legalist. He had the same wrong ideas Eliphaz had, as well as a similar approach. Job 8:20 records Bildad's summary statement: "God will not cast away the blameless, nor will He uphold the evildoers." Hmmm, sound familiar? "Job, you're in this mess because of your sin."

Yet Bildad took it even one step further. He said, "If your sons have sinned against Him, He has cast them away for their transgression" (Job 8:4). While Job was still mourning the loss of his children, Bildad suggests that the evil which befell them was the result of sin in their lives. Is that encouragement? And if so, who needs it?

ZOPHAR'S MISFIRE

Now it's Zophar's turn to encourage Job. He was like the young preacher who's never preached a sermon in his life, the young counselor who's never counseled anyone in his life—he had all the answers. He knew exactly what to say. Zophar was fond of one little expression which he used whenever he spoke. The Old Testament idiom is just exactly like it sounds today. Zophar always began his important speeches to Job by saying, "Know this." Isn't that great? "Know this, Job." You almost don't want to hear what follows.

I think Zophar gets the award for the most discouraging speech of the three. "Know therefore that God exacts from you less than your iniquity deserves" (11:6). In other words, "Job, if you think you're hurting, you ought to contemplate just how bad you'd feel if you *really* got what was coming to you." Job had lost everything, his life had disintegrated, he had nothing left but the breath in his mouth. And Zophar said, "Yeah, but if you knew how bad you really are, Job, you wouldn't be so angry right now. You're not even getting all the rotten things you really deserve."

That's encouragement?

HOW NOT TO ENCOURAGE

Job was accosted by three men who should have known better, three men who had lived long enough to realize that their observations couldn't possibly be accurate. But Job had to sit there and take it. The hurtful words of these three "friends" cause me to pray, "Lord, keep the Eliphazes, the Bildads, and the Zophars away from me should I ever have a Job day."

Yet we can learn something from these three men. We can learn how *not* to encourage someone who's in great pain.

1. Words without empathy

Job's friends were great encouragers for one week. They came to him, wept with him, and remained silent for seven days and seven nights. But after holding their tongues for a week, they spoke. And when their tongues were loosened, they accomplished precisely the opposite of what they set out to do (to encourage and comfort Job). They responded to Job's words but failed to feel his pain. In every one of the exchanges we find this pattern: Job speaks, sometimes in legitimate anger, and his "encouragers" respond to what he says. But every time they fail to see what's really going on in his life. They respond to his words, but they don't speak to his pain. In other words, they aren't really listening.

> "When a person is down in the world, an ounce of help is better than a pound of preaching."
>
> EDWARD GEORGE BULWER-LYTTON

Have you ever been talking with someone about a problem and all of a sudden you realize he's not really hearing you? He's thinking about how he's going to respond. He wants to be cute and clever in response to what has been said. But since he doesn't hear what was said, how can he be of any help in his answer?

It's so easy for us to generate words when we really haven't understood the problem, when we really haven't hurt with the person! The wisest thing Job's counselors did was to sit in silence with him for a week.

I have come to understand there is no formula which is readily prescribed, easily taken, or immediately successful for encouraging other believers. What we *are* to them is often far more important than what we *say*. How we sit and listen and are a part of their lives is often far more important than the words we speak.

In chapter 2 I mentioned Joseph Bayly, a man whose writings have helped me understand grief. He laid three of his sons in the grave. In one of his books, he wrote:

> I was sitting, torn by grief. Someone came and talked to me of God's dealings of why it happened, of hope beyond the grave. He talked constantly, he said things I knew were true. I was unmoved except to wish he'd go away. He finally did. Another came and sat beside me. He just sat beside me for an hour and more, listened when I said something, answered briefly, prayed simply, left. I was moved. I was comforted. I hated to see him go.[1]

We need to learn, as we try to help others, that encouragement may not be as much what we say as our willingness to be there in the moment of pain and to feel the hurt in the person's life. We need to know when to speak and when to be silent. Ruth Bell Graham, the wife of evangelist Billy Graham, understands the importance of silent encouragement. She wrote:

> Don't talk to me yet;
> the wound is fresh,
> the nauseous pain
> I can't forget
> fades into numbness
> like a wave,
> then comes again.
> Your tears I understand,
> But grief is deaf;

It cannot hear the words
you gently planned
and tried to say.
But...
pray...[2]

2. A poor theology of pain

The second mistake of Job's friends was their refusal to recognize suffering as a part of God's plan for Job. In the entire Book of Job, there is no evidence that these comforters understood that God had a positive and perfecting plan for Job which included these hardships. They looked for all the other reasons, because, like many modern theologians and counselors, they apparently believed there could be no godly reason for suffering, hurt, or pain.

But God *was* at work in Job's life. He had a purpose and it was a good purpose. Job, at the end, was a much better man than at the beginning. God perfected him. In addition to the contest between good and evil which centered *around* his life, there was also a perfecting ministry going on *within* Job's life, within his heart.

If we want to encourage people today who have been wounded, we must not start from the presupposition that Christians should not grieve, that Christians should not feel pain, that Christians should never suffer great trials or that Christians should not become deeply discouraged. Not are such presuppositions unrealistic, they are unbiblical. If we begin with these presuppositions, we come as "Job encouragers."

Many of the Psalms (and much of the rest of Scripture) are devoted to describing and encouraging believers whose backs are against the wall—believers enduring some kind of pain. The Bible is realistic about life. Suffering is inevitable. But the most important thing for any sufferer to understand is that God might be in his pain and hurt.

Think about how we usually pray for our brothers and sisters who are hurting. Let's be honest. Isn't our focus usually on the pain instead of the purpose behind it? And it doesn't help when influential teachers are advancing the success-prosperity philosophy of life.

Some years ago, I was given a book by Florence Bulle which bore this interesting title: *God Wants You Rich and Other Enticing Doctrines*. The author had some choice words for those who seek the easy way to growth and maturity.

> The deception in the success-prosperity doctrine is subtle. It sounds so spiritual to assert that we cannot be sick or fail if we trust God, and that He will reward us for faith and giving and being good, by making us rich in material things. But this was not the message of the men and women of faith who throughout history set church and nation aflame with revival.
>
> The more we pursue such poppycock, the more likely we will end up like pampered children. Getting everything we want won't turn us into soldiers for Christ. We may wear a tailored suit with gold buttons and hash marks, but we will be no more soldiers than the six-year-old with his feet shoved in his dad's old combat boots and carrying a wooden gun. Unchecked, the success-prosperity syndrome will not see Christians developing together into a vigorous, stouthearted, indomitable church. Rather, it will reduce the body of Christ to spiritual flabbiness.[3]

This past year I read that Jim Bakker, convicted in 1989 of defrauding PTL partners of millions of dollars, had been convicted once again. This time he'd been convicted by rereading and writing out every word in the Bible which Jesus ever spoke.

I had influenced so many people to accept a 'prosperity message,' I now felt that I had a responsibility to tell my friends what I had been learning from my studies of the Bible. I wrote a simple, straightforward letter and sent it to some of the people who had written to me in prison. In the letter, I told of the verses I had used improperly and what I had discovered by studying the true meaning of those verses. I apologized for preaching a gospel that emphasized earthly prosperity rather than spiritual riches. I wrote, 'I ask all who have set under my ministry to forgive me for preaching a gospel emphasizing earthly prosperity.' Jesus said, 'Do not lay up for yourselves treasures on earth.' He wants us to be in love with only Him.'[4]

One of the paramount lessons that we learn from Job's encounters is this: We must not assume what we could not possibly know. Only God knows the true purposes behind our pain.

3. Suffering equals sin

The third error Job's friends made was trying to relate all of Job's suffering to sin in his life. Technically, all suffering is due to sin. There wouldn't be any suffering if Adam hadn't disobeyed in the garden. All suffering is due to sin in that sense; but not all particular suffering is due to particular sin. Eliphaz, Bildad, and Zophar assumed all of Job's suffering was due to some particular sin in his life. And they were wrong.

It's possible to be a fine Christian and love God with all of your heart and still be depressed. Despite what you may hear and read from well-intentioned men, depression and despair are not necessarily the result of specific sin in a person's life. Some counselors will tell you to examine your heart and identify the sin in your life, confess the sin, and then you will be healed from your depression. While in some cases (where sin really is the problem) this is good counsel, in many instances it only serves to intensify the pain and confusion.

There are many clear biblical examples of men and women whose depression was not a result of particular sin. There's Moses—wandering in the desert, old, forgotten, and discouraged. And godly Hannah—downhearted, unable to eat, a victim of cheap remarks because she couldn't have children. And Elijah—fearful of his life, fleeing into the desert. These people were simply over-whelmed by the circumstances of life and felt discouraged and depressed.

I will never forget a conversation I had after one morning ser-vice at our church. A woman told me that when her mother died of cancer twenty years ago, a pastor declared that she died because she didn't have the faith to believe she could be healed, and because of sin in her life. The daughter lived with that destructive thought for many, many years. The pastor who gave that counsel was a modern Job's encourager.

4. All suffering is the same

Finally, Job's friends rejected the uniqueness of Job's suffering. They came with packaged, trite answers. They explained what was going on in Job's life based upon their own experience.

When God allows suffering to enter our lives, it is important that we use that suffering to help others. Second Corinthians 1:4 says, "We encourage others with the encouragement wherewith we ourselves have been encouraged." But we need to be careful not to assume we know exactly what others are feeling. Every experience of suffering is unique. There is no way we can know exactly how the person feels, for each suffering is specific to a particular time and a particular place and a particular set of circumstances.

In my years of pastoring, many people have said to me, "If one more person tells me they know what I'm going through, I'm going to scream!" Too often we come up with simplistic answers. We simply roll out Romans 8:28 and intone, "All things work together for good, you know." After the death of his father, a young boy asked me, "How can that be good? Tell me, how can that be good?" Sometimes what we need to say is simply, "I don't know. I just know that God in heaven is good." If we're going to be encouragers, real encouragers, we have to get past the misguided wisdom of Eliphaz, Bildad, and Zophar.

BACKSLAPPING NOT REQUIRED

We would do well to remember the words of the Lord when He finally interrupted Job's miserable counselors to ask a question: "Who is this who darkens counsel by words without knowledge?" (38:2). And we would be wise to consider the warning He issued to Eliphaz and his two friends: "My wrath is aroused against you and your two friends, for you have not spoken of Me what is right, as My servant Job has" (42:7).

If we wish to be godly encouragers, we will not speak until we have truly listened. We will not deliver pre-packaged answers. We will not pretend to know what we could not possibly know. And we will not point a finger...unless it is to direct our friend to the only true source of encouragement.

Remember, Christian encouragement does not require that we turn into backslapping, positive-attitude pep-talkers. Sometimes all it takes is to listen, to be present, to be quietly supportive. And then, if the right time presents itself, to gently recall that God is good, even when we don't understand. That's often enough. And it's always apt.

LOVE IN ACTION

Sometimes we discover that a major reason for our suffering has been what God intended to do in someone else's life. That may not be obvious to us. But Paul says that his sufferings were for the glory (or means of blessing) of others (Ephesians 3:13). He tells the Ephesians that they are not to lose heart because of his sufferings and imprisonment. Why? Because he believed that God had an evangelistic purpose in them. We know from his letter to the Philippians, written around the same time, what the purpose was.

> But I want you to know, brethren, that the things which happened to me have actually turned out for the further-ance of the gospel, so that it has become evident to the whole palace guard, and to all the rest, that my chains are in Christ; and most of the brethren in the Lord, having become confident by my chains, are much more bold to speak the word without fear (Philippians 1:12–14).

We do not always see the realization of God's purposes. None of us have the infallible ability to interpret God's perfectly wise purpose in the sufferings of our fellow believers (or of ourselves for that matter). But in order to encourage them, we need to have some awareness of what God may be doing. By sharing the biblical teaching on what God does in our lives through suffering, we may encourage others to serve God in it.[5]

IT'S UP TO YOU AND ME, FRIEND

IT'S UP TO YOU AND ME, FRIEND

Some time ago I came upon this delightful invitation. Read the words slowly to gain the greatest effect:

Come away with me on a little journey. We are about to behold the Master Artist at His easel. Before our very eyes, with brush in hand, He begins to stroke the canvas. The scene is one of a winter night as darkness is beginning to smother the earth. Heavy snowfall, tossed relentlessly by a vicious wind, blurs the vision as it sweeps across the landscape.

A chill sweeps over you as you see the trees, never before looking so lonely. Upon close inspection you begin to make out a large, isolated farmhouse, partially hidden in the trees. All is dark. As you study the work of the Artist, a feeling of loneliness grips your heart.

Even the ground, blanketed by snow, casts back only a dismal reflection. You begin to move away, when suddenly you notice the Master Artist once again taking His brush in hand.

From His palette He selects the choicest color of yellow, and with one stroke of the brush He fills the window of that farmhouse with light. What was once a picture of darkness and loneliness has been transformed into a cheerful light in the window.

What a picture of the church today! So many are so dark. In the night they almost disappear. And I'm not talking here about the discontinuance of the Sunday night services by so many local assemblies. I am talking about the failure of so many of our churches to bring light to the darkness of their communities. I think Marion Jacobsen has put her finger on the missing ingredient:

> If any group of Christians who claims to believe and practice all God has said in His Book will face up to their personal responsibility within the family of Christ, and to the real needs of Christians around them, their church will impress its community with the shining goodness of God's love—to them AND among them. Such a transformation probably would do more to attract others to Jesus Christ than any house-to-house canvas, evangelistic campaign or new church facility. People are hungry for acceptance, love and friends, and unless they find them in the church, they may not stay there long enough to become personally related to Jesus Christ.
>
> People are not persuaded, they are attracted. We must be able to communicate far more by what we are than by what we say.[1]

"Good words are worth much and cost little."
GEORGE HERBERT

It's true: People are not persuaded, they are attracted. They are drawn by the sense that something unique and dynamic is happening. If the light is really there, they can see it. In fact, some who have visited our church have told me that they can *feel* it! One couple expressed it to me in this way: "Pastor, my wife and I never feel more in love with each other and with God than when we stand in our church holding hands and worshiping God."

Unfortunately, it's not like this for everyone. People have actually said to me, "I go to church on Sunday, and it takes me all week to recover." That's not what God intended! God designed the church to be the place where people can be accepted for who they really are and be encouraged to become the people they were meant to be.

Ken Medema, the blind singer and writer, has a song which enjoyed more popularity in years past than it does today. But the message still speaks to the contemporary need of the local body of Christ. The title of the song is "If This Is Not a Place."

> If this is not a place where tears are understood,
> Then where shall I go to cry?
> And if this is not a place where my spirit can take wings,
> Then where shall I go to fly?
>
> I don't need another place for tryin' to impress you
> With just how good and virtuous I am, no, no, no,
> I don't need another place for always being on top of things
> Everybody knows it's a sham, it's a sham.
>
> I don't need another place for always wearing smiles
> Even when it's not the way I feel.
> I don't need another place to mouth the same-old platitudes.
> Everybody knows that's not real.
>
> So if this is not a place where my questions can be asked
> Then where shall I go to seek?
> And if this is not a place where my heart's cry can be heard,
> Then where shall I go to speak?

And if this is not a place where tears are understood,
Where shall I go, oh, where shall I go to cry?[2]

If the church of Jesus Christ is not a place where we can be who we are, where can we go? If the church is not a place where we can be encouraged and motivated throughout the process of our growth and maturing in the Lord, then where can we go to find such encouragement? If we are not known for our love for each other in the fellowship of the church, then what does that say about our status with God? "By this all will know that you are My disciples, if you have love for one another" (John 13:35).

Francis Schaeffer says this mark of Christianity ought to humble us and perhaps even frighten us:

It is as if Jesus turns to the world and says, "I've something to say to you. On the basis of my authority, I give you a right: You may judge whether or not an individual is a Christian on the basis of the love he shows to all Christians. In other words, if people come up to us and cast in our teeth the judgment that we are not Christians because we have not shown love toward other Christians, we must understand that they are only exercising their right which Jesus gave them.

And we must not get angry. If people say, "You don't love other Christians," we must go home, get down on our knees, and ask God whether or not they are right. And if they are, then they have the right to have said what they said.[3]

The Bible tells us clearly that the church, the gathering of believers, is to provide an environment of encouragement for all who seek it.

Let us consider and give attentive, continuous care to

watching over one another, studying how we may stir and stimulate and incite to love and helpful deeds and noble activities (Hebrews 10:22, Amplified).

Let us not neglect our church meetings as some people do, but encourage and warn each other, especially now that the day of His coming back is drawing near (Hebrews 10:25, TLB).

Therefore, encourage each other and edify each other, just as you also are doing. Now we exhort you, brethren, warn those who are unruly, encourage the fainthearted, uphold the weak and be patient with all (1 Thessalonians 2:11, 14).

I recently read a startling question addressed to pastors: "Do your sermons beat up or do they lift up?" Have you ever been in a church where you were beaten up from the pulpit and you walked out bruised? While it is true that we must preach against sin and declare the "whole counsel of God," the Bible admonishes us to make the local church a place where people can be encouraged and strengthened, not brow-beaten; a place where hurting people can find nourishment for their souls, not salt for their wounds.

Almost every week at our church, I meet folks who have come out of devastating church situations. They have been scarred, soiled, and manipulated. They're very thankful we don't pressure them into doing anything. They wander into our worship center, sit down in the pew, soak up the Word of God, and heal. And then perhaps some brother or sister in Christ will touch them with a word of encouragement, and little by little they will begin to once again sense God's wholeness in their lives.

The church needs to be a place where we can be built up and not beat up. The instruction (rather, the command) to encourage one another is found five times in the New Testament. It's addressed to all believers. It is not conditional. It is not optional. It's a command!

GOD'S BLUEPRINT FOR THE CHURCH

I'm afraid that for a lot of people, church is easily diagramed. They draw a line between the pulpit and the congregation. Everything important happens on the pulpit side of the line, and everything unimportant happens on the other side of the line. Some people get into the habit of coming to church to watch and to listen, thinking that the real action takes place behind the pulpit.

While it is true that many of us in the ministry have fostered this idea either by what we have taught or by the way we have functioned in leadership, God never intended such a dichotomy to exist between the clergy and the laity. The only real difference between a pastor and the people who sit in the pews is in function and gifts. While the pastor is a shepherd, he is also a sheep! We are all part of the same body, and we are to function together as one.

> For I say, through the grace given to me, to everyone who is among you, not to think of himself more highly than he ought to think, but to think soberly, as God has dealt to each one a measure of faith. For as we have many members in one body, but all the members do not have the same function, so we, being many, are one body in Christ, and individually members of one another. Having then gifts differing according to the grace that is given to us, let us use them: if prophecy, let us prophesy in proportion to our faith; or ministry, let us use it in our ministering; he who teaches, in teaching; he who exhorts, in exhortation; he who gives, with liberality; he who leads, with diligence; he who shows mercy, with cheerfulness (Romans 12:3–8).

You have just read God's original blueprint for the church. In his letter to the Romans, Paul outlined the dynamic ministry of the church "body." While the body is the whole church made up of all believers everywhere, in everyday practical operation, the body is the local church. The local assembly of believers is the place where the principles of body-life will be displayed and experienced. The invisible church, as the universal body is sometimes called, does not provide a very good venue for practicing encouragement.

Most of us are like the little boy who was afraid at night. When his father told him that God was with him, he replied, "Yes, but I want someone with skin on." We want to be encouraged by people we can see and touch. We need to be connected with real people who can understand us and love us and minister to us as we minister to them.

One of our small groups provided a great visual picture of this mutual ministry. A ball of yarn was used to demonstrate the interdependency of each member of the group. The first person took the end of the yarn and wrapped it around his finger. Then, looking at someone else in the circle, he affirmed that person and told him how much he appreciated and loved him. He tossed the ball of yarn to his brother and his brother wrapped the yarn around his finger and repeated the process of encouragement to another member of the group. This continued until there was a literal maze of yarn going in every direction back and forth across the span of that circle. This is what the church would look like if we could see it as God sees it!

> *"Oh give me a church Where the folks in the lurch Are encouraged and healed from above, Where seldom is heard A discouraging word, And the truth is modeled in love."*
>
> CHARLES R. SWINDOLL (TO THE TUNE OF "HOME ON THE RANGE")

THE IMMENSITY OF THE CHURCH

One of the primary motivations for a ministry of encouragement in the body has to do with its size. Paul mentions the church's immensity: "For we have many members in our body, and they do not have the same function, and so, we being many, are one body in Christ." Twice he refers to the "many" who are in the body. The body of Christ is made up of every believer in every place in this world. Everyone who has ever put their faith in Christ is baptized into the body of Christ (1 Corinthians 12:13). In other words, one is a member of the body of Christ if he is a Christian.

Many churches today have memberships in the hundreds or even thousands. One shepherd cannot be an encourager to hundreds or thousands of people. Nor is there a church staff big enough to provide the ministry of encouragement to such a massive number of people. God knows that! God never intended the pastor or the church staff to assume all the responsibility of encouragement. Because of the church's size—even a local church's size—each member must become an encourager. That's the only way it will work. And every time a person in the body says, "It's not my responsibility," someone, somewhere in the body isn't receiving the ministry God intended him or her to receive.

Here's how Reuben Welch captured the importance of this truth:

> You know something—
> we're all just people who need each other.
> We're all learning
> and we've got a long journey ahead of us.
> We've got to go together
> and if it takes us until Jesus comes
> we better stay together
> we better help each other.
>
> And I dare say
> that by the time we get there
> all the sandwiches will be gone
> and all the chocolate will be gone
> and all the water will be gone

and all the backpacks will be empty.
But no matter how long it takes us
we've got to go together.
Because that's how it is
in the body of Christ.

It's all of us
in love
in care
in support
in mutuality
we really do need each other.[4]

THE UNITY OF THE CHURCH

Like many of the great truths of the Bible, the words of Paul to the Romans are presented in such a manner as to preclude any distortion or misunderstanding. The concepts of body-life are held in tension one with the other. The immensity of the church is held here in tension with the unity of the church. "We being many are one body in Christ."

The second reason for reciprocal encouragement within the body is the oneness we share with each member. We are together. We all believe in Jesus Christ. The Holy Spirit indwells each of us. We are one in Christ. We're on the same team. And good team-members encourage each other.

When you watch a basketball game, you don't see opponents encouraging each other (at least, not until the game is over). Only players on the same team take the time to pat each other on the back and try to get each other fired up. It's normal and natural to encourage the people on your own team.

Paul was trying to help us understand (and we need to understand) that no matter what we look like or where we come from or what our background is or what kind of ethnic roots we have, if we have trusted Jesus Christ as our Savior, we are all on the same team! God only has one family! If we're in the family, we belong to Him. For that reason we ought to be patting each other on the back and cheering each other on toward the common goal of bringing glory to Jesus Christ, our Savior.

THE DIVERSITY OF THE CHURCH

Each of these aspects of the church are like different ingredients included in a recipe for some delicious dish. Each ingredient adds to the flavor of the final product. As Paul stirs the mix of body-life in the church, he now adds the element of diversity. "So we being many are one body in Christ and individually members one of another." And, "All the members do not have the same function."

Here's the beauty of diversity: Since each member in the body is different, experiences will vary. Because the most helpful encouragement usually comes to us from those who have been where we have been and experienced what we have experienced, think of the potential for support residing in each local assembly. Grace Noll Crowell expresses the value of such encouragement to one who has suffered loss:

> Let me come in where you are weeping, friend,
> and let me take your hand.
> I, who have known a sorrow such as yours,
> can understand.
> Let me come in—I would be very still
> beside you in your grief.
> I would not bid you cease your weeping, friend;
> tears bring relief.
> Let me come in—I would only breathe a prayer,
> and hold your hand.
> For I have known a sorrow such as yours,
> and understand.[5]

Because we all have different life experiences and walks with God, each of us has the potential for a unique ministry of encouragement. There are some people I can encourage because of the things I have experienced. There are some people you can really help because of what you have gone through. A single parent who has successfully raised children to adulthood can be a unique source of encouragement to someone just beginning the challenge of single parenthood.

Statistics tell us that some people in our churches are literally starving to death. Our church's "Food for the Hungry" program is constantly challenged to provide enough for those who are in need. Many single parents and their children do not have enough to eat. They need our help and encouragement. In your church there might be a teenage mother who is too embarrassed and ashamed to reach out for your help. There could be a teenage boy in trouble with the law and with school officials whose parents are trying to keep all this quiet because of shame, hurt, and fear. There's the divorced person who needs love and healing, as well as the married individual who comes alone, without the encouragement and Christian fellowship of his or her spouse.

Consider the sick and lonely one who's not enjoyed a personal visit or a loving touch in months, yet who has told no one. There's the father out of work with the unemployment checks about to run out...the visitor who's filled out a visitor card but doesn't feel at home and may never return...the person who carries the heavy pain and burden of a loved one's struggles with sin or sickness...the person who has a need so deep and so hurtful that not another soul knows...the person who is seeking but doesn't know Christ.

Friend, the ministry of encouragement cannot be left to a few pastors or deacons. It's an assignment that's been given to each member of the body. The goal of the church is to resurrect from within its members that deep, sometimes suppressed desire to help others, so that encouragement becomes the deserved reputation of the church.

THE INTERDEPENDENCY OF THE CHURCH

Fourth, the church's members are interdependent. "We are members one of another." We're not just members of the church, but members one of another. We have to relate to each other and we have to encourage each other. Because we need one another, we are truly dependent upon one another. Kent Hughes, who pastors the College Church in Wheaton, Illinois, grieves over the absence of this sense of interdependency:

> Church attendance is infected with a malaise of conditional loyalty which has produced an army of ecclesiastical hitch hikers. The hitch hiker's thumb says, "You buy the car, pay for the repairs, and upkeep and insurance, fill the car with gas—and I'll ride with you. But if you have an accident, you're on your own! And I'll probably sue." So it is with the credo of so many of today's church attenders: "You go to the meetings and serve on the boards and committees, you grapple with the issues and do the work of the church and pay the bills—I'll come along for the ride. But if things do not suit me, I'll criticize and complain, and probably bail out—my thumb is always out for a better ride."

Somebody has said there are two kinds of people in the church: the pillars and the caterpillars. The pillars hold the church up and the caterpillars crawl in and out every week. But for those who fail to get connected, there is a price to pay in needs that go unmet. John Naisbitt points out in his *Megatrends* that:

> The more technology we introduce into society, the more people will aggregate, will want to be with other people: movies, rock concerts, shopping. Shopping malls for example, are now the third most frequented space in our

lives, following home and workplace... You do not go to a movie to see a movie. You go to a movie to cry or laugh with 200 other people. It is an event.[7]

If I don't know who you are, how can I encourage you? If you don't know where I live or what goes on in my life, how can you touch my life? The pastor can try his best from the pulpit on Sunday, but if an individual determines to live in anonymity, there's not much the church can do to relieve his loneliness or minister to his pain.

THE RESPONSIBILITY OF THE CHURCH

Finally, Paul reminds us that his previous instructions were just that, instructions. Not suggestions, but marching orders! "Having then gifts differing according to the grace that is given to us, let us use them." Gifts are given to be used.

When I spoke to our church about encouraging "the write way," I had the privilege of watching as our members wrote encouragement cards even before they left the sanctuary. We decided that if ever there was a sermon that needed immediate application, this was the one.

Most of us have known that we need to be encouragers. But often what we know doesn't move us to action. We come, we sit, we listen, we agree with the message—and then what? Well, one Sunday we did something! I'm still hearing reports of what that one, simple act of love meant to so many in our community of believers.

GOOD ENCOURAGERS...

In the remaining verses of Romans 12, Paul outlines the lifestyle characteristics of godly encouragers. Take a moment to look them over.

1. Good encouragers have to be genuine

You can't be phony. "Let love be without hypocrisy" (12:9). Don't fake it. Be real.

2. Good encouragers are diligent

They're hard workers. "Not lagging in diligence, fervent in spirit, serving the Lord" (12:11).

3. Good encouragers are assertive

They take initiative. "Distributing to the needs of the saints, given to hospitality" (12:13). Do you know why many people are not encouraged? Because everybody thinks somebody else is doing the encouraging. And while we think somebody else is doing it, we take no aggressive action.

4. Good encouragers are selfless

They are concerned primarily for others. "Bless those who persecute you; bless and do not curse. Rejoice with those who rejoice, and weep with those who weep" (12:14–15). Good encouragers give themselves away to others.

F. W. Borham illustrated this concept beautifully:

The highest art in dominoes lies in matching your companion's pieces. Is he glad? It's a great thing to be able to rejoice with those who rejoice. Is he sad? It is a great thing to be able to weep with those who weep. It means, of course, that if you answer the challenge every time, it won't be long before your dominoes are gone. But it is worth remembering that victory in dominoes does not lie in accumulation, but in exhaustion. The player who is left with empty hands wins everything.[8]

Being an encourager takes something out of you. When you

weep with somebody, you've played your "weep domino" and it's gone. When you rejoice with somebody, they lay down a "rejoice" and you lay down a "rejoice," and for a little while your rejoice is gone. And pretty soon you've played all your dominoes—they're all gone. When that happens, you've won!

5. Good encouragers have a spirit of humility

"Be of the same mind toward one another. Do not set your mind on high things, but associate with the humble" (12:16). Often we look to encourage only those people who are "at our level." For example, if we're professional people, we'll encourage professional people. But what about the homeless person who walks in and sits down next to us? What about the unlovely person? The shabbily dressed person? Do we find it hard to reach out with encouragement to these people?

THE ENCOURAGING CHURCH

A true encourager is authentic in who he is. He's a hard worker who's assertive in reaching out to people. He's not fearful because he's selfless and primarily interested in others. He is unaffected by any sense of class-consciousness. To him, a person is a person, no matter who he might be.

The following contemporary song has always reminded me of my personal responsibility to be a source of encouragement wherever I go:

> Two doors down one rocking chair is rocking
> She sits there all alone, her husband dead and gone
> The best years of her life they spent together
> He was always strong, but now she's on her own.
> And the telephone never rings,
> No one laughs, No one sings,
> It's quiet there, Does anyone care?

A knocking at the door breaks the silence
She looks out to see, the little boy from down the street
She cracks the door surprised that he came over
Flowers in his hand, like a little gentleman
He said I picked these just for you,
Hope you like the color blue
I could stay awhile, I love to see you smile.

It only takes a little time
To show someone how much you care
It only takes a little time
To answer someone's biggest prayer.
Light your world
Let the love of God shine through
In the little things you do
Light your world
And though your light may
Reach only two or three
Light your world.[9]

LOVE IN ACTION

Some of the most quotable ideas I've ever seen were produced anonymously. That's the case with the following "Ten Commandments of Friendship," which I consider choice advice for anyone desiring to fulfill the biblical mandate of encouragement. Read these wise instructions and see if you don't agree.

The Ten Commandments of Friendship

ONE: *Speak to people.* There is nothing as nice as a cheerful word of greeting.

TWO: *Smile at people.* It takes 72 muscles to frown, but only 14 to smile!

THREE: *Call people by name.* The sweetest music to anyone's ear is the sound of their own name.

FOUR: *Be friendly and helpful.* If you would have friends, be friendly.

FIVE: *Be cordial.* Speak and act as if everything you do were a real pleasure.

SIX: *Be genuinely interested in people.* You can like everyone IF YOU TRY.

SEVEN: *Be generous with praise, cautious with criticism.* Try for a ratio of seven praises to each criticism.

EIGHT: *Be considerate of the feelings of others.* It will be appreciated.

NINE: *Be thoughtful of the opinions of others.* People love their opinions as they do their own children; calling them ugly won't get you anything but anger.

TEN: *Be alert to give service.* What counts most in life is what we do for others!

ABOUT THE AUTHOR

Dr. David Jeremiah is the founder of Turning Point, an organization committed to providing Christians with sound Bible teaching relevant to today's changing times through radio and television broadcasts (nationally and internationally), the Internet, compact-disc series, and books. Dr. Jeremiah's teaching covers a variety of topics including the family, grace, spiritual warfare, and biblical prophecy.

Dr. Jeremiah lives in a suburb of San Diego, California, with his wife, Donna. They have four children and numerous grandchildren. He serves as senior pastor at Shadow Mountain Community Church in El Cajon, California.

In 1982, Dr. Jeremiah wanted to bring the same solid teaching to San Diego television that he shared weekly with his congregation. Shortly thereafter, Turning Point expanded its ministry to radio. The *Turning Point* program is currently heard or viewed around the world on radio, television, and the Internet in English. *Momento Decisivo,* the Spanish translation of Dr. Jeremiah's messages, can be heard on radio in every Spanish speaking country in the world. The television broadcast is currently seen throughout the Middle East through METV and Kingdom Sat.

Because Dr. Jeremiah desires to know his listening audience, he travels nationwide holding "A Night of Encouragement" radio rallies. According to Dr. Jeremiah:

"At some point in time, everyone reaches a turning point, and for every person, that moment is unique, an experience to hold onto forever. There's so much changing in today's world, it's difficult always to choose the right path. Turning Point offers people an understanding of God's Word as well as the opportunity to change the direction of their lives."

Also from David Jeremiah

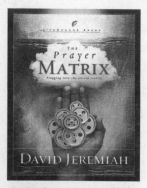

The Prayer Matrix

David Jeremiah approaches the good news of God's willingness to respond to our prayers from a fresh angle, describing prayer as the built-in trigger for the good things that happen in this world. Readers will discover just how eagerly God is waiting to answer us. Like a loving father, He is always glad to have us come to Him as children with the things that are on our heart! Prayer delights God's heart, because He has ordained the processes of the world to work through the prayers of His people.

978-1-59052-181-6

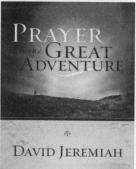

Prayer, The Great Adventure

We all know how important prayer is and how it affects our daily lives. However, we don't exercise our privilege to pray to our heavenly Father often enough. In this inspiring rerelease, Dr. David Jeremiah addresses the challenges we all face and the answers to prayer we often miss. God's blessings require a relationship that is fostered through prayer. Drawing from his personal prayer journals, Dr. Jeremiah shares his heart—both blessings and struggles—to provide insights that teach us how to embark on the most satisfying of trips, the great adventure of prayer.

978-1-59052-182-3

CHAPTER ONE:
WHAT THE WORLD NEEDS NOW

1. Karl Menninger, *Whatever Became of Sin?* (New York: Hawthorn Books, Inc., 1973).

2. Dr. Eric Berne, *Games People Play* (New York: Grove Press, 1964), 14.

3. Dr. S. I. McMillen, *None of These Diseases* (Westwood, N.J.: Fleming H. Revell, n.d.), 79–80.

4. Edwin Markham, "outwitted" in *Anthology of the World's Best Poems* (memorial edition) (New York: W.H. Wise, 1948), 265.

5. Source unknown.

CHAPTER TWO:
EVERYBODY IS A SOMEBODY

1. Webster's New Collegiate Dictionary (Springfield, Mass: G & C. Merriam col, Publishers, 1959), 271.

2. William Barclay, *New Testament Words* (Philadelphia: Westminster Press, 1964), 221, 222.

3. E. F. Schumacher as quoted in Richard A. Swenson, *Margin: How to Create the Emotional, Physical, Financial and Time Resources You Need* (Colorado Springs: NavPress, 1992), 26.

4. Jeremy Rifkin as quoted in Richard A. Swenson, *Margin: How to Create the Emotional Physical, Financial, and Time Resources You Need* (Colorado Springs: NavPress, 1992), 26.

5. Richard A. Swenson, *Margin: How to Create the Emotional Physical, Financial, and Time Resources You Need* (Colorado Springs: NavPress, 1992), 39–40.

6. Dietrich Bonhoeffer, *The Cost of Discipleship,* trans. R. H. Fuller, Rev. Irmgard Booth, rev. ed. (New York: McMillan, 1959), 16–17.

7. As told by Jeanne Doering, *The Power of Encouragement: Discovering Your Ministry of Affirmation* (Chicago: Moody Press, 1982), 164–165. Used by permission.

8. Bill and Gloria Gaither, "Because He Lives," (Gaither Music Co., 1971). Used by permission.

CHAPTER THREE:
A RESURRECTION OF HOPE

1. Stuart McAlpine, *The Road Best Traveled* (Nashville: Thomas Nelson Publishers, 1991), 290.

2. Bill and Gloria Gaither, "Because He Lives," (Gaither Music Co., 1971). Used by permission.

3. Stephen Hopper, "onesiphorus: A Refresher Course," *Discipleship Journal,* 1 September 1986, Vol. 34, 5–6.

CHAPTER FOUR:
WHEN ALL ELSE FAILS

1. Jean Fleming, *Finding Focus in a Whirlwind World* (Dallas: Roper Press, 1991), 73.

2. Elisabeth Elliot, ed., *The Journals of Jim Elliot* (Old Tappan, N.J.: Fleming H. Revell Company, 1978).

3. G. Campbell Morgan, "Jubilation in Desolation," *The Westminster Pulpit*, Vol. 6 (Westwood, N.J.: Fleming H. Revell, n.d.), 147.

4. William Martin, *A Prophet with Honor* (New York: William Morrow and Company, Inc., 1991).

5. Ibid.,

6. J. Oswald Sanders, "How to Rise Above Discouragement," *Discipleship Journal*, Issue 28, July 1, 1982, 4–7.

CHAPTER FIVE:
FRIEND THERAPY

1. John W. Drakeford, "Hugs," *The Awesome Power of Positive Attention,* (Nashville: Broadman Press, 1990), 151.

2. Paul Borthwick, "Sink or Swim: Your Ministry of Encouragement," *Discipleship Journal*, Issue 54, Nov./Dec. 1989, 8–11.

CHAPTER SIX:
MR. ENCOURAGEMENT

1. Jack Canfield and Mark Victor Hansen, *Chicken Soup for the Soul* (Deerfield Beach, Fla.: Health Communications, Inc., 1993), 213.

2. H. Stephen Glenn and Jane Nelsen, *Raising Self-Reliant Children in a Self-Indulgent World* (Rocklin, Calif.: Prima Publishing & Communications, 1989), 83–84.

3. Quoted from Alan Loy McGinnis, *The Friendship Factor* (Minneapolis: Augsburg Publishing House, 1979), 100–101.

CHAPTER SEVEN:
THE ENCOURAGEMENT ZONE

1. Anonymous author.

2. George Bernard Shaw, quoted in *The Portable Curmudgeon*, ed. Jon Winokur (New York: New American Library, 1987), 191.

3. F. Herwaldt, "The Ideal Relationship and Other Myths About Marriage," *Christianity Today*, April 9, 1902, 20–21.

4. F. S. Pittman, "Beyond Betrayal: Life After Infidelity," *Psychology Today*, May/June 1993, 32–38.

5. Dwight Hervey Small, *Design for Christian Marriage* (Westwood, N.J.: Fleming H. Revell, 1959), 32.

6. Dr. Robert B. Taylor, "Behind the Surge in Broken Marriages," *U.S. News and World Report*, (22 January 1979), 53.

7. *The Holy Bible: The New King James Version* ©1984 by Thomas Nelson, Notes, 11.

8. Ken Canfield, "Father's Greatest Gift," *New Man* 54.

9. R. Kent Hughes, *Disciplines of a Godly Man* (Wheaton, Ill.: Crossway Books, 1991), 35–36.

10. Dwight Hervey Small, *Design for Christian Marriage*, (Westwood, N.J.: Fleming H. Revell, 1959), 35.

11. Richard Selzer, *Mortal Lessons: Notes in the Art of Surgery* (New York: Simon and Schuster, 1976), 45–46.

12. Jerry D. Twentier, *The Positive Power of Praising People* (Nashville: Thomas Nelson Publishers, 1993), 190–191.

CHAPTER EIGHT:
CHILDREN NEED CHEERLEADERS

1. Barbara Dafoe Whitehead, "Dan Quayle Was Right," *The Atlantic Monthly,* (April 1993), 47.

2. Christopher N. Bacorn, "Dear Dads: Save Your Sons," *Newsweek,* (7 December 1992), 13.

3. Robert Rains, *Creative Brooding* (New York: MacMillan Co., 1966), 81–82.

4. *The Works of John Wesley,* Vol. 1 (Grand Rapids, Mich.: Zondervan Publishing House, 1972), 386.

5. David Jeremiah with Carol Carlson, *Exposing the Myths of Parenthood* (Dallas: Word, 1988), 11.

6. Ruth Stafford Peale, *The Friendship Factor*.

7. Tom Bisset, *Why Christian Kids Leave The Faith* (Nashville: Thomas Nelson Publishers, 1992).

8. "Opinion Legislation," Unpublished work by Brennan Bagwell and Scott Elkins. Used by permission.

9. Steve Farrar, *If I'm Not Tarzan & My Wife Isn't Jane, Then What Are We Doingin the Jungle* (Portland, Ore.: Multnomah Press, 1991), 93.

10. Bruce Larson, *The One and Only You* (Dallas: Word Books, 1974).

11. Jerry D. Twentier, *The Positive Power of Praising* (Nashville: Thomas Nelson Publishers, 1994), 126–127; 129–130.

CHAPTER NINE:
THE WRITE WAY TO ENCOURAGE

1. Charles Colson, *Loving God* (Grand Rapids: Zondervan Publishing House, 1983), 209–216.

2. Ibid., 273.

3. Ibid.,

4. Ibid.,

5. Jerry D. Twentier, *The Positive Power of Praising People* (Nashville: Thomas Nelson Publishers, 1994), 20–24.

CHAPTER TEN:
WITH FRIENDS LIKE THESE...

1. Joseph Bayly, *The Last Thing We Talk About* (London: Scripture Union, 1973), 40, 41.

2. Ruth Bell Graham, as quoted in Elizabeth Skoglund, *Wounded Heroes* (Grand Rapids: Baker Book House, 1992), 200.

3. Florence Bulle, *God Wants You Rich and Other Enticing Doctrines* (Minneapolis: Bethany House, 1983), 41.

4. Jim Bakker, *I Was Wrong* (Nashville: Thomas Nelson Publishers, 1996), 540–541.

5. Dr. Sinclair Ferguson, "Just Being There," *Discipleship Journal,* Issue 24, July 1, 1985, 22–25.

CHAPTER ELEVEN:
IT'S UP TO YOU AND ME, FRIEND

1. Marion Jacobsen, *Saints and Snobs* (Wheaton, Ill.: Tyndale House Publishers, 1972), 67.

2. Ken Medema, "If This Is Not a Place," copyright 1982, Glory Sound Music Co. Used by permission.

3. Francis Schaeffer, *The Church at the End of the Twentieth Century*, 137.

4. Reuben Welch, "We Really Do Need Each Other," copyright 1976 by Impact Books, a Division of the John T. Benson Co. Copyright reassigned in 1982 to The Zondervan Corporation. Used by permission.

5. Grace Noll Crowell, "To One in Sorrow," Source unknown.

6. R. Kent Hughes, *Disciplines of a Godly Man* (Wheaton, Ill.: Crossway Books, 1991), 152.

7. John Naisbitt, *Megatrends* (New York: Warner Books, 1982), 45.

8. Frank W. Boreham, *A Bunch of Everlastings* (Philadelphia: The Judsen Press, 1949).

9. "Light Your World," by Eddie Carswell, M. Aramian, Oliver Wells, and Nile Borop, copyright 1989 Causing Change Music and Dayspring Music (a div. of Word, Inc.)/BMI, Tallulah Tunes and World Music (a div. of Word, Inc.)/ASCAP, Wella Music/ASCAP and NB Music/ASCAP. Used by permission.